The Theatre Student

STAGE VIOLENCE

The Theatre Student

STAGE VIOLENCE

Albert M. Katz

Illustrations by
Gary Finelli

Photographs by
Peter G. Blank

PUBLISHED BY
RICHARDS ROSEN PRESS, INC.
NEW YORK, N.Y. 10010

Published in 1976 by Richards Rosen Press, Inc.
29 East 21st Street, New York, N.Y. 10010

First Edition

Manufactured in the United States of America

Library of Congress Cataloging in Publication Data

Katz, Albert M
  Stage violence.

  (The Theatre student)
  Bibliography: p.
  1. Stage fighting. I. Title.
PN2071.F5K3   792'.028   75–28392
ISBN 0–8239–0336–2

For Harry
and Esther

ALBERT KATZ grew up in mid-Manhattan in a time when the ten-cent subway fare and the $1.20 matinee ticket made it possible for a young boy to see Broadway plays as easily and frequently as motion pictures. The theatre proved irresistible, and he started working with community and school theatre groups at age thirteen. He has been involved with educational, community, and professional theatres ever since.

Dr. Katz received a bachelor's degree at Union College in Schenectady, New York, and master's and doctor's degrees at the University of Michigan, in Ann Arbor. Since 1960, his primary focus of attention has been in the area of university teaching and directing. He has taught at the University of Michigan and Alma College (Michigan), and since 1966 has been Director of Theatre at the University of Wisconsin at Superior.

He is a founder and the first president of the Wisconsin Theatre Association and a member of the Board of Governors of Region III in the American Theatre Association. He has published numerous articles, including the one in *Players Magazine* that was the genesis of this book.

Dr. Katz has had a special interest in stage violence for many years, partly, as he says, out of a sense of self-preservation. Many of the violent techniques he describes in this book, he learned growing up in the streets of New York. He is quick and grateful to point out that he learned much more as an observer than as a participant. When he first encountered violence on the stage, he began employing his street knowledge to keep from getting hurt, and quickly found that these techniques

translated easily to the stage, providing "flash" and illusion as well as safety. Over the years, Dr. Katz has taught workshops in stage violence and staged combats for professional, community, and educational theatres in New York, Connecticut, Ohio, Michigan, Indiana, Illinois, Minnesota, and Wisconsin. Stage violence is a regular course at the University of Wisconsin at Superior.

The accumulated experience of the years has been distilled and gathered in this book. From the first, the idea has always been the same: "Make it look good . . . make it exciting . . . make it illuminate character . . . and then *walk away from it without a scratch!*"

ACKNOWLEDGMENTS

My deep appreciation to Denise Breider, who managed to read my handwriting; to Matt Cetnar, Patty Myette, Jeff Nelson, and Margot Ruckstein, who put in many hours modeling for photographs and illustrations; to William and Claribel Halstead, who taught me most of what I know.

Selection from *Rashomon* by Fay Kanin and Michael Kanin reprinted by permission of William Morris Agency, Inc.

CONTENTS

About the Author   7
Acknowledgments   9
Foreword   17
Preface   19

Part I
Falling: The Foundation of Violence

I.   How to Fall   23
     The Basic Theory of Falls—Kinesthetic Learning   23
     Execution   24
       Side-falls   25
       Front-falls   27
       Back-falls   27
         Variations of Side-falls   27
         A Sit-down Fall   27
       Falling to Your Knees   28
II.   Self-motivated Falls   30
     Fainting   30
     Tripping   31
     Medical Seizures   32
     Drunk Falls   32
     Slapstick and Pratfalls   33

Part II
The Planning and Execution of Violence

III.   Body Blows, Unarmed   37
     The Theory of Isometrics   37
     Slapping   40
     Punches   43
     Use of Other Parts of the Body to Deliver Blows   44
IV.   Head Blows, Unarmed   48
     The Theory of Delivering Head Blows   49
     Punches to the Head   49
     Use of Other Parts of the Body   50
V.   Wrestling and Unarmed Martial Arts   52
     Theory of Wrestling for the Stage   52
     Application and Use in Stage Wrestling   52

	Judo and Wrestling Throws	*53*
	Hip-rolls	*54*
	Arm-throws	*59*
	Leg-drops	*62*
	Weapon Disarms	*64*
	Weapon Exchanges	*65*
	Karate and Judo Blows and Martial Arts	*66*
	What not to do, and why	*66*
	What you can safely do, and how	*67*
	Special Techniques for Women	*67*
	Hair-pulling	*68*
	Scratching	*68*
	Choking	*69*
VI.	*Knife Handling*	*72*
	Theory and Practice for the Stage	*72*
	How to Hold and Handle the Weapon	*73*
	Creating the Illusion of Stabbing and Withdrawal of the Weapon	*76*
	Physiological Action and Reaction to Being Stabbed	*78*
VII.	*The Use of Weapons*	*81*
	Theory and Practice for the Stage	*81*
	Body Blows	*82*
	Head Blows	*83*
	The Choosing of Weapons	*83*
	The Historical Period	*83*
	The Nature, Social Class, and Purpose of the Character	*85*
	Gentlemen's Rules vs. Battlefield or Street Conditions	*86*
VIII.	*Swords: Technique and Application for the Stage*	*89*
	Danger: Flying Steel	*89*
	The Difference Between Competition and Stage Fencing	*91*
	Stance and Position	*92*
	Cut, Thrust, and Parry	*97*
	Disarms	*104*
	Offensive and Defensive Arcs	*109*
	Rhythmics and Structure	*111*
	Choreography and Kinesthetic Learning	*111*
	Warmup and Practice	*112*
	Consistency in Weapons	*112*
	Maintaining Weapons	*112*
IX.	*The Use of Weapons, Shields, and Armor in Stage Combat*	
	Swords	*114*
	One-hand Swords, Used with a Shield	*114*
	Long Two-hand Swords	*115*
	One-hand Swords Used Alone	*117*
	Shields and Armor	*117*
	Use for Defense	*118*
	Use for Offense	*120*

	Spears and Polearms	*122*
	Crushing—Impact Weapons	*126*
X.	*The Handling of Firearms*	*130*
	Safety Procedures	*130*
	Choosing and Using the Weapon	*132*
	Body Awareness on the Part of the Actor	*133*

Part III

Choreography of Conflict

XI.	*The Nature and Techniques of Choreography*	*137*
	The Technical Procedures of Planning and Noting Choreography	*137*
	Choreography for Character and Mood	*142*
	Comic Mode	*145*
	Serious Mode–Naturalistic	*149*
	Serious Mode–Stylized	*154*
	Choreography as an Instrument of Revelation	*155*
	Summary	*158*
	Appendix. Some American Suppliers	*160*
	Bibliography	*160*

ILLUSTRATIONS

Chapter I—*How to Fall*   23
  Figure 1.   Side-fall   25
  Figure 2.   Side-fall   26
  Figure 3.   Front-fall   26
  Figure 4.   Back-fall   27
  Figure 5.   Sit-down back-fall   28
  Figure 6.   Falling to your knees   29
Chapter II—*Self-motivated Falls*   30
  Figure 7.   Tripping yourself   31
Chapter III—*Body Blows, Unarmed*   37
  Figure 8.   Isometric neutrality in full-body use   39
  Figure 9.   Slapping   42
  Figure 10.   Righthand body blow   44
  Figure 11.   Right knee to body   45
  Figure 12.   Right clbow to body   46
Chapter IV—*Head Blows, Unarmed*   48
  Figure 13.   Head blow   50
Chapter V—*Wrestling and Unarmed Martial Arts*   52
  Figure 14.   Isometric grappling in wrestling   53
  Figures 15 and 16.   Backward hip-roll   55
  Figures 17, 18, 19, and 20.   Forward hip-roll   57
  Figure 21.   Forward arm-throw or lock   59
  Figure 22.   Forward arm-throw, Step 4b   60
  Figure 23.   Rear arm-lock   61
  Figure 24.   Backward arm-throw, Steps 1, 2, and 3   61
  Figure 25.   Backward arm-throw off a hip-roll, Step 4a   62
  Figure 26.   Backward arm-throw off a leg-drop, Step 4b   62
  Figure 27.   Forward leg-drop   63
  Figure 28.   Backward leg-drop   63
  Figure 29.   Defensive leg-drop   64
  Figure 30.   Scratching   69
  Figure 31.   Choking   70
Chapter VI—*Knife Handling*   72
  Figure 32.   How to hold a knife   74
  Figure 33.   The illusion of stabbing, Steps 1, 2, and 3   77
  Figure 34.   The illusion of stabbing, Steps 4 and 5   77
Chapter VIII—*Swords: Techniques and Application for the Stage*   89
  Figure 35.   Square-on body position   93
  Figure 36.   Side-to-side body position   93

Figure 37.   Light sword grip   94

Figure 38.   Heavy sword grip   94

Figure 39.   Foot position—neutral guard, square-on   95

Figure 40.   Foot position—attack guard, square-on   95

Figure 41.   Foot position—defensive guard, square-on   96

Figure 42.   Foot position—side-by-side position   96

Figure 43.   "The Pass"   97

Figure 44.   Proper angle and position of a weapons clash   99

Figure 45.   Sword grip for a backhand cut   99

Figure 46.   Parrying with a shield   101

Figure 47.   Parrying with a blade: overhead parry   102

Figure 48.   Parrying with a blade: shoulder parry   102

Figure 49.   Parrying with a blade: flank parry   103

Figure 50.   Parrying with a blade: "gate" parry   103

Figure 51.   Blade disarm: dagger, left hand   105

Figure 52.   Blade disarm: sword, right hand   106

Figures 53 and 54.   Blade disarms: sword, right hand   107

Figure 55.   Blade disarm: sword, right hand   108

Figure 56.   Blade disarm: sword, right hand   109

Figure 57.   Flight-path arc of a right flank cut   109

Figure 58.   Arc ratio of 4:1—safe choreography   110

Chapter IX—*The Use of Weapons, Shields, and Armor in Stage Combat*   114

Figure 59.   Overhead parry with a two-hand broadsword   116

Figure 60.   Square-on polearm grip (depicting a shoulder cut and parry)   124

Figure 61.   Polearm overhead parry   125

Figure 62.   Polearm trip, between legs   125

Figure 63.   Battle-ax disarm   127

FOREWORD

This book is designed for the uninitiated . . . for all the amateurs in the best (and original) sense of that word . . . the lovers of theatre, who have not had the benefit of formal training in stage violence.

Those of you who have had professional training in gymnastics, tumbling and fencing will find much that you already know. I think you will also find some new and additional material, some different perspectives, that may prove helpful. To the degree that you do, this book is meant for you, too.

For the rest of us, however, the dedicated amateurs and many of the professionals in the civic and community theatres, the public schools, and the colleges and universities, that depth of training was not available. We have to stage violence in the theatre, and we don't know how to begin.

The book was written on the premise that the reader is wholly ignorant of the techniques in question. In many cases this will not be true. But I have started each unit from "Step 1" for safety's sake, because that is the primary purpose of the book. With the ideas and concepts that follow, you should be able to have it both ways: to create excitement on your stage and safeguard your actors. Use them in good health . . . that's the whole idea, isn't it?

PREFACE

Stage violence is a very tricky and complex art, the application of which all too often leads to bruises, scratches, and abrasions when one is lucky, and to serious injury when one is not. Although almost all directors and teachers stress their sincere concern for the safety and well-being of their actors, stage violence is often carelessly prepared by the director, carelessly rehearsed by the performers, and then executed with prayer rather than precision. Sometimes the cast gets away with it. They may have a sequence of action that shows more enthusiasm than theatrical effectiveness, but at least nobody gets hurt. Sometimes they do not get away with it, and then someone is hurt.

First of all, one should define the term "stage violence." It includes, but is not exclusively made up of, various forms of armed and unarmed combat. It also includes any action that requires an actor to strike another person, an object, or the floor. Thus it encompasses the performance of faints, trips, pratfalls, medical seizures, and "practical jokes" just as surely as it does formal fighting. Whenever actors must ricochet off each other or some hard surface, they are engaged in stage violence. By this standard, "violence" is widespread in our dramatic literature. Every actor and every director will come in contact with it if they work in even a few plays. Yet how much is known about the techniques of stage violence, in terms both of safety and of theatrical effectiveness? How much information is available? The answer, unfortunately, is very little.

Stage combat is very exciting and glamorous. It is a great deal of fun to stage and to perform. But all stage violence from the simplest comic pratfall to the bloodiest mass battle scene is serious business. Neither the director nor the performers should ever forget that fact. They should never "play" with violence as a spontaneous or casual thing. Young actors, particularly, tend to be careless and coltish about stage violence unless warned severely against it. There is something utterly intoxicating about fight scenes, and especially about swords, in the hands of amateurs. There is the overwhelming urge to impersonate Errol Flynn, and it is only after a blunt blade has nonetheless achieved enough velocity and torque from an exuberant swing to slash a cheek or an arm, or a completely buttoned point on a fencing foil has nonetheless pierced an eye or torso, that a terribly frightened actor or cast suddenly realizes that these are tools of the stage, not toys! A piece of stage violence must never be played with; it must be performed. In the realm of stage violence, hands, feet, elbows, and knees are all deadly weapons, all as capable of inflicting injury as a club, knife, sword, or axe.

When conceived with an inventive eye and a sound sense of character; when

19

approached with professional care, exactitude, and respect; when prepared and practiced with patience and energy, stage violence is a marvel! It can and should be the highlight of a scene or of an entire play. It can bring forth gales of laughter or whoops of excitement, gasps of surprise or stunned silence, in perfect safety for all performers.

Part I

FALLING: THE FOUNDATION OF VIOLENCE

Chapter I

HOW TO FALL

THE BASIC THEORY OF STAGE FALLS— KINESTHETIC LEARNING

All modes of violence (comedy, medical, self-motivated, and combat) have a tendency to resolve themselves with a performer falling to the floor. The problem faced by the performer and the director is how to accomplish this safely.

If a director instructs an actor simply "to fall," rather than teaching him how to fall; if, as an actor, you simply "let yourself go" and trust to providence and the resilience of youth instead of learning how to fall, you are risking serious injury to your back, kneecaps, wrists, fingers, and/or the ball-socket joints of your shoulders. In the case of back-falls you are risking skull fracture. You are all but guaranteeing a series of unnecessary bruises and floor burns.

It is relatively easy to learn how to fall safely. By "safely" I mean precisely that: no bruises, no scratches, no abrasions, no floor burns. It is not enough to walk away from a fall, or a series of falls, without requiring medical attention. A performer should be able to rise and walk away from any type of fall, and any number of rehearsals of that fall, without having experienced pain.

At this point I think the concept of *kinesthetic learning* needs to come into play. The idea of "learning by doing" is as old as education, and begins as early as the infant's acquisition of the ability to talk, walk, and function in the world around him.

Every time you do something, you imprint a slight groove on your brain and set a very light layer of potential habit into your musculature. When you repeat the action, the mental groove is deepened, and another layer of the muscular behavior pattern is set in. When you have practiced an action often enough, the mental signal pattern for the sequence of mini-actions that make up the whole becomes thoroughly ingrained, completely accurate, and subject to instantaneous recall. The intensively repeated layers in the sequence of muscular actions impelled by these mental signals become "laminated" into a powerful sequential bond, inseparable, and almost incapable of being scrambled.

From the seemingly simplest of actions, such as lifting a forkful of food to your mouth, to the rather complex, such as driving a car with a four-speed manual transmission, you have already mastered thousands of instances of kinesthetic learning, for that is what each of these tasks involves.

Do you think it is simple to eat? Watch a baby learning to manipulate strained apricots from his dish to his mouth with a spoon. Messy, isn't it? He misses the dish with his spoon. He forgets to open his mouth. Then he opens it, but misses his mouth with the apricots. Then he miscalculates the spatial relationship involved and knocks the dish off the high-chair tray. Look again. Do you realize the incredible number of sequential muscular actions that must be accomplished by his shoulder, arm, wrist, and fingers, all guided and coordinated by his eyes and mind, to accomplish that simple act of eating? Hundreds of miniactions are involved. No wonder the child has so much difficulty. But we have done it now for anywhere from sixteen to sixty years and have some millions of kinesthetic imprints in our minds and musculatures. We have learned kinesthetically so that we do not think of it at all, we just do it. Our sibling, our child, our grandchild . . . they are first learning now. We think it's funny. They think it's maddening. They're right! Watch them learning and you will learn, too.

Does that example seem too remote? Do you still think that learning isn't all that kinesthetically oriented? How many of you have learned or tried to learn to drive a car with a manual transmission? Remember the first few times? Buck . . . buck . . . stagger . . . sputter . . . stall! Again and again you jerked into motion, got the gear shift in the wrong position, tangled your feet on the wrong combination of two out of three pedals and the car sputtered to a halt, hopefully without hitting a tree or a pedestrian, while all the time your instructor tried to keep on smiling but really approached a state of coronary arrest.

You handle that car quite smoothly now, but have you forgotten what it was like to learn? Of course it was difficult. You had to manipulate simultaneously and in a coordinated fashion an accelerator, a brake and a clutch using only two feet; you had to handle a gear shift, a steering wheel, and turning signals, using only two hands; you had to keep track of traffic, pedestrians, traffic signals, and the speedometer with your two eyes. And while all this was happening your instructor was talking to (yelling at?) you, giving you helpful hints and instructions. You were in sensory overload, my friend, and, unless you were very unlike the vast majority of your fellow human beings, you blew it . . . you "spilled your apricots all over the floor."

You *wanted* to learn, though. It was important to you. So you tried again, and again, and again until you could get it down, get it

right. Now when you drive, you still handle three pedals with two feet, keep your hands and eyes in constant motion, judge traffic, and make dozens of instantaneous decisions each minute. Yet your conscious mind is free to do anything else you want it to: make a shopping list, solve a math problem, or engage in a political argument with your passenger. You are an experienced driver, and you have worked your mind and body through the gear box thousands of times and it's second nature to you now. You have learned it to the point where you do not have to think about the action, you just do it! That is kinesthetic learning . . . and that is the state you want to arrive at with any and all stage violence you prepare for a given production. You must practice it, on a safety mat, until it is second nature. The secret of dramatically successful and physically safe stage violence is carefully choreographed planning combined with diligent and repeated practice. Kinesthetically learned stage violence works! Kinesthetically learned stage violence is safe.

Now, let's start with falls.

EXECUTION

There are three basic rules to follow, regardless of the type of fall being learned:

1) All falls must be learned and practiced on mats to protect yourself while you learn.

2) Falls must be practiced again and again, on the mat, until they can be safely accomplished instinctively and as a matter of reflex. Then they must be rehearsed off the mat, so that you become used to the hard surface that you will have to perform on.

3. You must make sure that there is nothing in your pockets or on your person that will break or that will injure you. No keys, no wallets, no pencils, and no glasses can be in your pockets. Keys are sharp and hard; they will penetrate the skin and cause a gash at worst and a bad bruise at best. A thick wallet full

of "junk" will cause a deep bruise on your hip. Glasses in your pocket may break. A pen or pencil can become a lethal weapon forced into your body. Glasses on your face can fly off. Rings on your fingers can hurt, and a wristwatch may be broken. (I once had occasion to do a side-fall with a pipe in the tool pocket of my jeans. The resulting painful bruise took two weeks to disappear.)

Only when the falls described in this chapter are part of the performer's repertory are you ready to incorporate the techniques of falling into the acting and action of a role.

Falls can be divided into three categories: 1) side-falls; 2) front-falls; and 3) back-falls.

1) Side-falls (for a fall to the right)

Side-falls are based on the modern dancer's side-fall. The basic technique involves making the first floor-contact with the calf muscle instead of the kneecap, and then rippling the body down segment by segment:

Step 1) Stand with feet parallel and shoulder-width apart. Shift your weight to your right side and roll your right foot over sideways. (Keep weight completely to the side, not at all forward. If you cannot be perfectly sideways oriented, favor a backward tilt rather than a forward tilt).

Step 2) Flex your knees and allow your body to relax downward and to the right. First contact will be with the right calf. (Your hand and supporting arm should not yet have made contact with the floor).

NOTE: Most performers have a tendency to feel more secure if they tilt or lean just a bit forward. This is a basic error, because leaning forward will cause you to come down on the edge of your kneecap instead of on the calf muscle. That Hurts! Lean back instead. The mat will protect you both from psychological insecurity and from the consequence of error.

Step 3) Continue free fall and make contact with side thigh muscle.

Step 4) Continue free fall and make contact

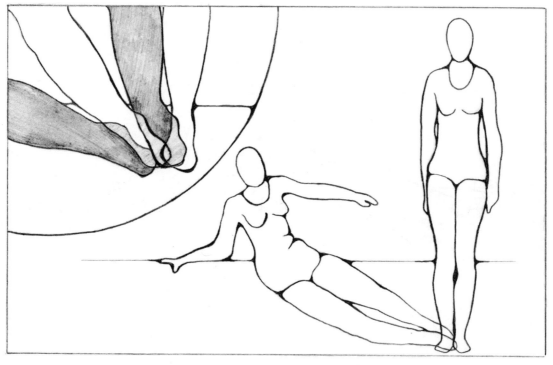

Figure 1   Side-fall

Figure 2   *Side-fall*

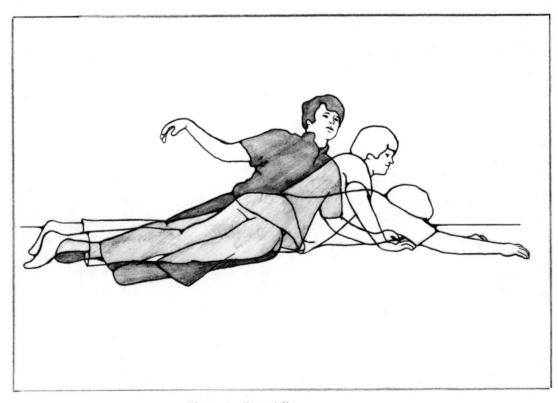

Figure 3   *Front-fall*

with side of hip. At this point your right hand should make contact with the floor at a 45-degree angle, in line with your ear, and provide additional support. Do not slam your hand onto the floor. Do not use the hand as a brake. Simply accept the second point of support and allow it to slide in the direction your body is already going.

Step 5) Meanwhile, arch your rib cage sideways to the right. Try to flex it like a bow. Continue your fall and roll (do not "crash") onto your rib cage. Your hand will continue to slide.

Step 6) You are now completely prone. You are in contact with the floor from the side of your foot to your shoulder to the palm of your outstretched hand. Do not brake yourself suddenly at this point, but allow yourself to roll over on your back and to continue to roll, easily and freely, until your momentum is played out.

2) Front-falls

Steps 1 to 4 are the same as for side-falls.

Step 5a) Arch your back. Try to flex it like a bow. Your stomach & chest come forward. Then, twist your torso and roll from your hip onto your stomach.

Step 5b) As you roll onto your stomach, thrust your legs out behind you.

Step 5c) As you come over onto your stomach, slide both hands in front of you, in contact with the floor, and allow them to keep sliding.

Step 6) This step is the same as for side-falls.

3) Back-falls

There are two types of back-fall. The first is modeled on the side-fall:

Steps 1 to 4 are the same as for side-falls.

Step 5a) Tuck your head so that your chin touches your collarbone.

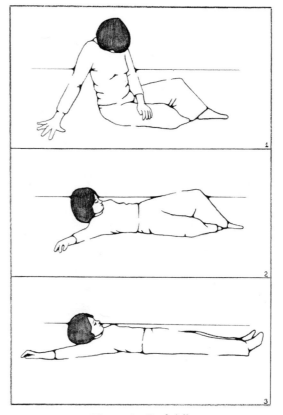

Figure 4   *Back-fall*

Step 5b) Roll over on your back.

Step 5c) Continue to slide your hand in the direction your body is going.

Step 6) This step is the same as for side-falls.

The second type of back-fall is a variation of the common everyday action of sitting on your heel:

Step 1) Stand erect with your feet parallel and your balance evenly distributed.

Step 2a) (*for practice only*) Slide one foot backward 14 to 16 inches and sit down on your heel, maintaining your balance. You have already done this at a party or around a campfire a hundred times. Do this action several times until you are comfortable with the movement.

Step 2b) (*for accomplishing the back-fall*) Slide one foot backward 14 to 16 inches and

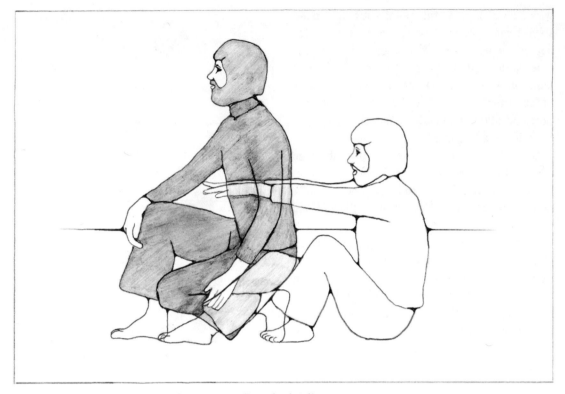

Figure 5 *Sit-down back-fall*

sit down on the floor, *behind* the heel. You will find that you can maintain your balance until you are over and past the heel of your shoe, and that you are reaching the ground with your buttocks after a "controlled crash" from a height of approximately 6 to 8 inches.

Step 3) Tuck your chin so that it touches your collarbone.

Step 4) Roll over onto your back.

Step 5) As you do Steps 3 and 4, take the arm on the same side as the foot you have slid backward, and arc it over your head to slap the palm hard onto the floor about the same time as your shoulders touch the floor. This provides both braking action and the sound your head would have made if it had hit the floor.

Step 6) Same as for all other falls, "roll out the momentum."

Notes: 1) The reason for the fall will indicate the proportion of downward thrust (or sag) to the proportion of sideways thrust. This will tell the performer how much momentum needs to be "rolled out." For example, a ladylike faint will call for practically none at all, whereas a vicious shove will call for a great deal.

2) The person taking the fall always provides his own momentum. Although another performer may need to simulate the reason for the fall, that person must never actually do so! If an actor is knocked over he is, by definition, off-balance and vulnerable to accident. If the actor takes himself down, he is on balance and in control of his own body.

4) *Falling to your knees*

If you must fall to your knees, do not crash downward, because the kneecap is vulnerable and easily injured.

Step 1) The center of weight and balance is

the pelvis; therefore bring your pelvis forward directly over the balls of your feet. Your feet should be 4 to 6 inches apart.

Step 2) Tighten your buttocks and bring your weight down and forward until your toes are gripping the floor for balance and you are just about sitting on your heels.

Step 3) Lean your weight forward on, and then over, your toes until you have placed your knees on the floor.

Note: Swaying your shoulders and head backward as you do this will provide compensatory balance and allow your torso to remain comfortably upright as you complete the move.

SUMMARY

Do not underestimate the importance of starting with these basic techniques. As we progress through the chapters on self-motivated falls and various additional types of mayhem, you will find that each of them (with the exception of slapping) leads to the same result: the person on the receiving end winds up on the stage floor. Unless you have practiced the falls until you have learned them kinesthetically, to the point that you can do them safely as a matter of reflex, you have two choices:

a.) You can take your mind and concentration off of the character and/or situation that has created the dramatic tension of the scene and resulted in the violence, and focus on doing the fall correctly, which is bound to hurt the dramatic effectiveness of the scene; or . . .

b.) You can stay in character, react to the

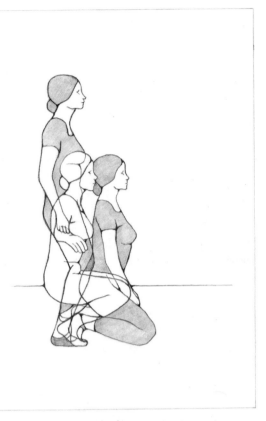

Figure 6   *Falling to your knees*

blow with full motivation and take your chances on getting hurt.

When there has been sufficient kinesthetic learning, when your body is sufficiently trained so that you are secure, intellectually and emotionally, in your own ability to handle the fall, then neither of the two above options need apply. You can stay in character and react with full motivation, secure in your own ability to carry out the action without risk to yourself, to others, or to the production.

Chapter II

SELF-MOTIVATED FALLS

Self-motivated falls may derive from fainting, illness, or drunkenness. They may also be caused by tripping over an object, over a person, over one's own feet, or by the performer's being (theoretically) struck by an object such as a rock or a bullet.

FAINTING

The simplest of self-motivated falls is the faint. Magda faints at the sight of the police-inspector in Act III, Scene 1, of Menotti's *The Consul.* In *Bye Bye Birdie,* the girls faint en masse at Birdie's appearance. Anastasia faints at the end of Act I, in *Anastasia.* The list is endless. Faints abound in dramatic literature for men and women, for young and old.

The factors to be taken into account are 1) the impetus of the fall and the consequent roll-out; 2) the character's reason for the faint; and 3) the physiology involved in fainting.

As far as impetus is concerned, there is none. A basic premise of a faint is that no one else is physically involved. Another character may have given you the emotional and/or motivational reason for fainting, but no one has struck you, pushed you, etc. In terms of both audience illusion and physical reality, you fall to the floor because you have lost consciousness. The basic technique is a side-fall, or a front- or back-fall off of a side-fall. There should be no roll-out because there is no impetus. You collapse straight down. Never simply "let yourself go" and fall to the floor. Your body must be in total control all the way down. Simple as it may look, never do the initial practice sessions on a hard surface. Always learn the faint on a mat. Only when you are secure in the move should you try it on the hard stage floor. Conversely, be sure that you rehearse the faint numerous times on that hard stage floor, so that you are accustomed to it before you attempt to integrate it into an overall rehearsal.

The second factor of character motivation is interrelated with the physiology of fainting (the reason you are fainting). The cause may be terror, surprise, drug- or alcohol-related lightheadedness, grief, pain-related shock, loss of blood, hyperventilation, etc. Each of these causes will lead to a loss of consciousness at a different rate of speed, so that the collapse may be gradual or sudden. Depending on the cause, your musculature may be anywhere on the scale between relaxed and tense in the last moment before your character loses consciousness. The thing to remember is that people fall when they faint because their bodies have relaxed completely and simply are not holding them up. However tense your character may have been in the split second before the faint begins, a transition is aesthetically, physically, and physiologically necessary and proper from that state of tension to one of complete relaxation so that you are *ready* to fall. This is what happens to the body in real life. It is also the proper state to be in to achieve a safe fall.

In summary, then:

Step 1) Know *why* you are fainting.

Step 2) Know the state your body is in at the moment before you faint.

Step 3) Take a transition, where necessary, from the state of tension in Step 2 to a state of complete physical relaxation.

Step 4) Take yourself down by a side-fall and come to rest on your side, front or back, whichever you wish, with little or no roll-out.

Step 5) Practice the faint on a mat until you are perfectly secure with it and can do it kinesthetically, without having to think about it.

Step 6) Practice the faint on the stage floor until you are kinesthetically secure.

Step 7) Don't integrate a faint into the overall context of the scene until steps 1 through 6 have been accomplished.

TRIPPING

Tripping is usually followed by a fall to the floor, although this is not necessarily the case. You can catch yourself against a wall, a piece of furniture, a set-piece, or another actor. In any case, you do not want to be out of control when you hit the floor or the object or person catching you. Whatever the motivation for the "trip," whatever the audience illusion is meant to be, in reality you must "trip" yourself so that you can maintain balance. This will prevent potential damage to yourself, your partner, and the stage setting.

There are two basic categories of trips. In the first, you stumble or trip all by yourself, over a board, a step, a piece of furniture, or your own feet. In the second, you are tripped, deliberately or accidentally, by another person. In the latter situation, your partner's tripping action must be illusory, not real. He must place his foot where it seems you have tripped over it, but you should never make contact with his foot. In that way, you are not in danger of actually losing your balance.

The technique of creating the trip is fairly simple. As you move forward in a normal stride, jam the toe of your trailing foot into

the heel of the lead foot. This will provide the jerky interruption of the forward movement, and "throw" you forward into your fall. If you wish to go down in a left-side fall, then your left toe should trail behind and jam into the heel of your right foot. For a right-side fall, trail your right toe into the heel of your left foot. Falling toward the side of your trailing foot provides the better balance and control.

Figure 7 *Tripping yourself*

Step 1) Jam the toe of the trailing foot into the heel of the lead foot. (*See Figure 7.*)

Step 2) As you start to "pitch forward" your weight naturally goes onto the lead foot.

Step 3) Swing the heel of your trailing foot outward, by pivoting on the ball of that foot. This will put the calf muscle in position to make the first contact with the floor. A large or tall person may wish, instead of pivoting

pratfalls are all variations of the faint and the trip. Each of these derives from one of the falls discussed in Chapter I. In almost all of the falls arising from these conditions, several rules pertain:

1) Make sure you practice your fall, whatever its motivation, on a mat until you are kinesthetically secure.

2) Make sure you practice your fall, out of context, on the hard stage floor before integrating it into the context of the scene.

3) Make sure you have adequate open space in which to accomplish the fall without danger of striking a set-piece or furniture on your way down.

4) Make sure that nothing about your costume or personal properties interferes with the safety of the fall. There must be nothing in your pockets to stab or bruise you on the side on which you are falling. For example, a necessary personal prop can be placed in your left pants pocket or the left pocket of your suit coat if you know you will be executing a right side-fall. Are you wearing a sword? Carrying a knife? Get rid of it before you fall, or make sure it is adequately sheathed and that you fall away from it.

5) All falls are done on your own. Another actor may provide the motivation for the fall by pretending to strike, trip, or shove you, but it must be only a pretense. You take your own fall, provide your own momentum, and always keep your own balance. The moment you accept an actual impetus, a real push or trip or shove, you have given up control of your balance. At that point you cannot guarantee control of your body, and you are risking injury.

6) The director has the ultimate responsibility for the safety of his actors. If a situation is dangerous, the director should modify the conditions so as to make them safe. If a director refuses to make the modifications, the actor should refuse to take the fall!

Part II

THE PLANNING AND EXECUTION
OF VIOLENCE

Chapter III

BODY BLOWS, UNARMED

Up to this point we have been working with self-impelled, self-motivated violence. Everything done in Chapters I and II is done by the performer with, at most, the illusion of interplay with a partner. We now get into external violence, where at least two people are involved, with one dealing the blow and the other receiving it. External violence involves direct contact such as slapping, punching, and the use of elbows, knees, feet, the head and the torso. Also involved are wrestling and, of course, the use of weapons; these two problems will be taken up in detail in later chapters.

Is there anyone reading this page who has not seen more "action" plays, films, and television shows than he can remember? Whether it be Westerns, police stories, detective stories, or war stories, the examples are the same. In these plays and films, the hero and the villains always tangle at least once and usually several times. The number of blows dealt and received is large and their nature enormously varied. I have seen John Wayne hit in the stomach with a 2″ x 4″ beam, grunt a little, and then mutter in his inimitable fashion, "All right you polecat [he never uses strong language, just violence], now you've got me mad!" Wayne "shakes off" the effect of the blow in about three seconds, while his opponent conveniently waits for him to do so, and then proceeds to wreak righteous vengeance upon his foe (who may be waiting in sheer surprise that "Duke" ever got up!).

Have you ever been hit in the stomach with a 2″ x 4″? Or with a baseball bat? I do not recommend it! It can crack ribs, rupture in-

ternal organs and, in general, be very messy! What, then, has happened? The camera is very close. You can see these large, well-muscled men swinging at each other with all their strength. Blows are rained on the head and body of the victim with any part of the assailant's body that is available, or with any object ready at hand. It can't be real, or they would run out of actors very quickly. They are skillfully creating the illusion of violence—but how? The blows are delivered in a similar fashion regardless of their source (fist, knee, elbow), and vary more in relation to their target than to their origin. Blows to the head are delivered in one way, and we shall deal with this in the next chapter. Blows to the body are handled in another way. Body blows should always be based on the theory of isometrics.

THE THEORY OF ISOMETRICS

According to the dictionary, something that is "isometric" has "an equality of measure." A number of years ago "isometric exercise" was very much in fashion. The idea was simple and practical. If you tensed sets of muscles in opposite directions, you would offset each set of muscles with the other and could "exercise" at your desk without having to use a lot of space or expensive equipment. If you clasp your hands together palm to palm with your fingers locked and pull with 50 pounds of force with each hand, then you are truly exerting 100 pounds of pressure, but neither hand will move. You will have 50 pounds of pull to the right, 50 pounds of pull to the left, real exertion and exercise, and no movement, because you have "zeroed out" the pressure at the point of contact. That is the principle we are applying. Let us see how it works on stage.

The techniques of delivering and reacting to body blows on stage can be summarized in three sentences:

1) Any blow, any reaction to a blow, can be divided into its component parts.

2) The muscular action of each part can be determined.

3) The muscles in that action can be set in isometric opposition, canceling each other out so that a blow which involves full muscular effort nevertheless lands with little or no genuine impact.

Let us say, for example, that you are trying to hold a door closed against a large and vicious enemy. If you are genuinely trying to do this, then:

Step 1) You use the floor as a launching pad for your body. Your feet are pressed against the ground, thrusting downward with maximum effort to hold your body against the door.

Step 2) Your calf muscles are tensed to their maximum, pressing downward.

Step 3) Your thigh muscles are also straining in a lifting mode, pressing downward against the launching pad.

Step 4) Your buttocks muscles, among the most powerful you have, are in the same "set."

Step 5) Your ankles, knee joints, and hip joints are locked to form a continuous column of support with your spine to thrust upward against the door.

Step 6) Your entire torso is aligned under your shoulders, and all muscles are straining in the same direction, against that door.

Step 7) Your arms and hands are tensed, either continuing the column from your back and shoulders, or in support of the shoulder(s) pressed against the door.

In sum, every part of your anatomy is aligned to drive upward and outward against that door, and you are putting the maximum pressure you can into the effort, let us arbitrarily say 200 pounds of pressure.

There is a problem with this, however. On stage, that door is made of light wood and canvas. The flats are lashed or loose-pin hinged together. If you really put 200 pounds of pressure on the stage door, you will tear it from its hinges, or you might take the whole stage set down with your ferocity.

You do have an alternative, of course. You can pretend to exert energy and force, but in reality keep some of your muscles slack. Most actors who try this solution press hard with their hands and engage their shoulders, but relax from the waist down so that there is no base of support. The problem here is that you will get caught by your audience. Most people in a moderate-sized proscenium house will be able both to see and to sense (from what your breathing and the cords and veins on your neck are *not* doing) that you are faking it. In an intimate proscenium house, and in an arena theatre where the audience is right on top of you, you can be certain that they will catch you faking it. So . . . that won't work!

Well, if you can't actually use your full strength against the door without destroying the set, and if you can't fake it without destroying the illusion of effort and strain, then what can you do? You can use isometrics. You can divide the sets of muscles and portions of your anatomy into opposing camps so that instead of 200 pounds of thrust against the door you have 100 pounds of thrust going up and out toward the door, and 100 pounds of thrust going down into the floor, with the fulcrum of balance being in the same portion of your anatomy where it has always resided in your body: the pelvis. The pelvis *is* the fulcrum, the center of balance in the upright human being. Standing, running, jumping, dancing, whatever the action, your center of balance is always the pelvis. Try this in pantomime, against a "door" of thin air . . . it works!

Step 1) Your feet are flat on the floor, but your toes are gripping and *lifting,* as though trying to resist being picked up instead of pressing against the floor, using all the gripping power you can get.

Step 2) Your calf muscles are tensed in a lifting mode, pressing downward.

Step 3) Your thigh muscles are flexed to their maximum, trying to draw your knees together. Thus they are using horizontal thrust, not a vertical lifting thrust.

Step 4) Your buttocks are tensed, but they are being pulled downward, as though you were pulling something heavy down to you from up above.

Step 5a) Your ankle joints are locked in support of the gripping action of your feet.

Step 5b) Your knees are slightly bent and are not locked; and you are using the strength of those joints, with their tendons, to resist the muscle pressure from your thighs to·bring your knees together.

Step 5c) The ball-socket hip joints are reacting and swiveling as necessary to take up the torque of adjusting the conflicting muscle and joint pressures of steps 1 to 5b. (At this point, assuming 100 pounds of pressure is being generated from your feet to your hips, roughly 15 pounds is being generated inward horizontally by your thigh muscles pressing both down and in; 15 pounds is being generated outward horizontally by your knees resisting that pressure; roughly 35 pounds is being generated upward against the door by your calves; and roughly 35 pounds is being generated downward by your hips and feet in their gripping action. The figures are arbitrary, but the principle is not. The result is a net thrust of zero pounds against that door . . . from the lower half of your body.)

Step 6a) Your entire torso is set to the task of expanding. Stretch your rib cage. Press against it as much as you can, trying to enlarge your air capacity and press your breath hard against it. All of this effort is now radiating outward, on a horizontal plane. The effort *is* real so it *looks* real, but it has no bearing on whether that door stays open or shut (net result: zero pounds of pressure against that door).

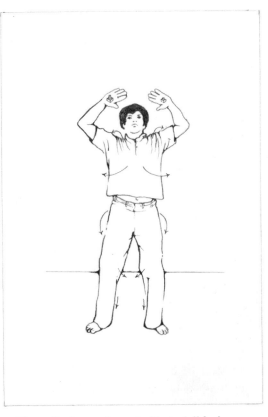

Figure 8 *Isometric neutrality in full-body use*

Step 6b) Line your spine up under your shoulders and pull against the door with your shoulders trying to open it.

Step 7) Your arms and hands are divided as follows: forearms and hands straining against the door trying to keep it shut; and biceps mediating between forearms, hands, and shoulders, taking up whatever slack is needed to "zero out" this particular isometric tension.

(Net result: zero pounds of pressure against that door).

Please note that you have engaged every muscle, tendon, and skeletal support structure in your body in the service of this action. You are exerting yourself to your utmost, and that effort will be conveyed to the audience. The theatrical illusion of the effort expended to keep that door shut will be absolute, because it is not an illusion. You are working terrifically hard. Yet all that effort, all 200 pounds of thrust, is self-contained by isometric action, and you are putting no pressure on the set. This allows you to use the technique with a fragile box-set, or even in an arena situation with a door made of 1″ x 2″ framing and an audience 18 inches away.

This basic technique of isometrics applies not only to holding doors shut. It applies to wrestling, judo, and all types of body blows. We will put it to that use in a few pages, but, first, the techniques of slapping.

SLAPPING

As the ladies already know, and some of the gentlemen may have found out, a slap can do a lot of damage, particularly if it is well placed and the wrist is cracked at precisely the right moment. That may make good self-defense, but it makes for poor performance technique. Your goal is to make maximum sound and minimum contact at the point where it will have maximum theatrical effect and cause minimum physical discomfort and *no* damage.

A slap is one of the most common acts of physical violence between two characters in dramatic literature. Men slap women, women slap men; women slap each other and so do men. Large people slap small people and vice versa. Slaps occur in tragedy, melodrama, domestic comedy, and farce. They are so common that people tend to take them for granted, whereas they are actually rather dangerous. There are two types of solutions,

and each one brings with it its own danger.

The first solution is the "You can take it, kid" approach, in which the performer slaps his partner full in the face because that is what the character is supposed to do. The person receiving the blow is supposed to accept the resulting pain and/or physical damage as the price of "being in the theatre." This is just plain stupid!

The cheekbone is pretty fragile, and if the person delivering the blow is fairly large and/ or strong, or happens to get a good snap of the wrist as the blow is delivered, then the person on the receiving end is likely to wind up a) in great pain; b) in a very tenuous state of consciousness; with, c) a badly shaken state of focus and concentration on ensuing lines and business; and d) a fractured or shattered cheekbone; or e) any combination or all of the above. If the blow lands over the ear, and particularly if this procedure is repeatedly rehearsed, then one can add the distinct possibility of hearing loss to the above list.

At the 1974 American College Theatre Festival regional presentations in Milwaukee, one of the productions was an original script entitled *Tricycle Sunshine*. It is a particularly sadistic script, which includes an inordinate amount of "beating up" on the actress playing the title role of Sunshine. At one point in the production, she "zigged" when she should have "zagged" and the hinge of her jaw was torn loose. I was informed that she would spend the next six weeks with her jaw wired, taking liquids through a straw. This kind of thing is totally unnecessary. I do believe that you need to make contact with your partner in order to achieve the desired dramatic effect, but there is a specific technique available, described below, which allows you to do that while minimizing physical discomfort and eliminating the danger of injury.

The second solution is the "Now you see it, now you don't" theory, in which the slap misses the recipient's face and head entirely, and lands on a) the recipient's hand, which has been brought up alongside the face; b) the assailant's hand, which has just been used on the recipient's face to "position it" for the slap, and is therefore in the correct position; or c) thin air, with the slapping sound being provided by the person being slapped, or another actor on stage, clapping his hands together. This is a good idea. It is certainly safe. The problem is that it practically never works aesthetically.

In talking to actors, directors, and audience members I have gained an all but unanimous impression that the performers are constantly getting caught at the deception. In cases "a" and "b" above, the audience sees where the blow lands and sees the second hand getting into position to receive the blow. (If you try to snap the hand into receiving position at the last second, the timing of it is likely to misfire). The audience may accept this as a "convention" and not object too much. However, a slap usually occurs at a climactic moment of a scene, or of an entire play. When you have built your audience up to this moment, when they have entered into the dramatic growth of tension leading to this release of violence, then this is the last moment you want to shatter the illusion with a badly faked slap.

If you try option "c" you have a terrible dilemma. You either have the recipient provide the sound, or you have to have a third person on stage to produce the sound. Where do you put this third person? If you put him across the stage from the blow, then the audience will clearly hear that the sound came from someplace other than the place where the blow was supposed to have landed. If you place him right next to the person receiving the blow, even facing upstage, the audience will at least see the movement of his shoulders, arms, and back as he produces the sound. The movements of the recipient's hands and arms have the same effect. There goes your illusion again. Try to split the difference, and have "the third man" close but not too close, so he won't be seen—near, but not too near, so that

the sound will seem to come from the right place? You can't do it! The likely result will be the audience's both seeing *and* hearing the true origin of the sound, just as they would if the recipient provided the action.

All right, the script calls for a slap. You can't hit without risking damage, and you can't miss without shattering the illusion. What can you do? You *can* hit. You can hit pretty hard, although the assailant is never free just to swing away with all his strength. The trick to a dramatically effective and physically safe slap lies in how you hold your hand when you slap, and in where the slap lands:

Step 1) Cup your hand as though to drink water from the palm. If your hand is flat you will make maximum contact. If your hand is cupped, there is a hollow in your palm and you will make minimum contact even though you are striking with your whole hand. In addition, the hollow of the palm will provide a louder and more resounding sound effect than the actually more damaging blow struck with the flat palm.

Step 2a) *Where* do you hit your partner? Do not strike him on the cheek. It hurts a lot, and you may fracture the cheekbone. Do not strike him over the ear. It hurts a lot, and you may cause ear damage and/or a hearing loss. The neck muscles are specifically designed by nature to be the "shock absorbers" for the head, to cushion impact. Of course it will sting. The skin will probably redden with the second blow. It will certainly redden with the third blow if you are swinging hard enough to be theatrically effective. The point is that while your partner will feel the blow, it will not *hurt*. It should be well below the level of tolerance that your partner can take without losing concentration or being in pain. The feeling is much more akin to being clapped on the shoulder than to being slapped in the face, yet it provides the latter effect.

Step 2b) Ideally, when delivering the blow, your thumb should be aligned with and just

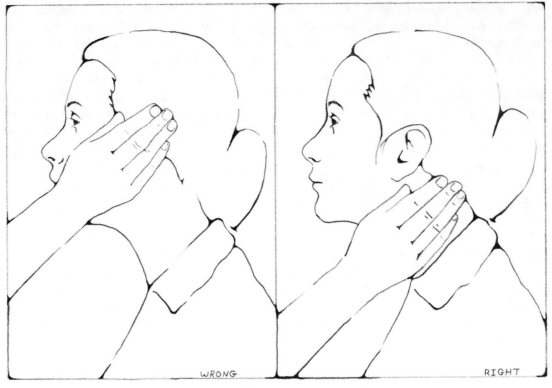

WRONG   RIGHT

Figure 9 *Slapping*

underneath the side of your partner's jawbone, and the rest of your hand (with the hollow cupped palm) should be covering the *hollow* of your partner's neck that curves in from the jaw, so that only the top and bottom of your hand make contact with his neck. This hollow-to-hollow contact provides a very loud and effective "pop" in terms of sound and the absolute minimum of contact. Follow through on your contact so that your hand slides off the victim's neck, and finishes the full arc of the blow.

Step 3) Check your distance, arc of swing, and placement of hand very carefully. Practice in slow motion six to ten times before swinging full speed. If you can't land exactly on target (with your thumb in alignment with his jaw), then it is better to land low than high.

Step 4) Get the slapping sequence set early in rehearsal, and practice it at every rehearsal. Both of you need to get used to it and

to be comfortable and familiar with the blow. This will avoid surprises, flinching, or miscalculation in performance.

Note:

1) How hard the assailant can swing will be determined by common sense and by the relative size and strength of the assailant and the recipient. A 110-pound girl can take a pretty good whack at a 250-pound male recipient if she lands in the right place. The reverse is obviously not true. A large actor playing Othello will have to restrain the force of the blow he aims at a slight Desdemona.

2) None of this will work, of course, if the actors do not trust each other, and if they are not deserving of trust. There must be no "games-playing" with the rehearsal of this business. They must follow the procedure. If the arc of the blow is changed and it lands on the face, we are back where we started. The same is true if the recipient ducks either out

of the way of the blow, or worse still, straight into it with his face.

PUNCHES

Punches to the body are "pulled" by means of "isometric" muscle use. When you are actually trying to do damage, all of your muscles are coordinated to deliver the maximum foot-pounds of impact in one direction, toward and into the target. Let us assume you are righthanded and wish to deliver a punch to the stomach. You will stride forward on your left foot (for both velocity and balance) and swing your right arm. Your whole body, from the balls of your feet, through your legs and hips, your torso, your shoulders and arm, will be coordinated to drive the right fist into the target with as many foot-pounds of impact as you can muster. All of your effort is forward, into the target, with X foot-pounds of impact.

When you are on stage, you are attempting to create the illusion of damage. If you apply the principle of isometrics to this, your goal will still be to employ X foot-pounds of effort, and still to employ your entire body and musculature. However, you will be putting various sets of muscles in opposition to each other so that "½X" foot-pounds of effort are being thrown forward into the target, and "½X" foot-pounds of effort are being pulled back away from the target. Thus, ideally, when your fist reaches your partner's stomach, he is struck with zero foot-pounds of impact. The opposition of the two sets of muscles has canceled both out. The illusion of the impact, however, is enormous because you have really engaged your entire body in the action and to maximum effect.

Let us return to the specific example of the righthand blow to your partner's stomach:

Step 1) You stride forward on your left foot and your right leg is into the blow.

Step 2) Your left leg, starting with the ball of your left foot, is dug into the ground as a brake, instead of pushing off to add impetus.

Step 3) As you swing your arm, your hips rotate left and thrust forward with your movement to balance out the opposing muscular action of your two legs.

Step 4) Your right arm is accelerating forward as hard as it can.

Step 5) Your right shoulder is acting as a brake (your arm and shoulder muscles are opposed, and are canceling each other out.

Step 6) Your torso, which is very flexible, rotates left with the blow. There is a balance here that each performer will have to find for himself, but in a "ripple effect" of the torso muscles, the lower part of the torso supports the forward thrust of the hips. The upper part of the torso, particularly on the right side, supports the braking action of the right shoulder.

Step 7) The left arm is free either to grasp your partner or to swing backward for balance.

In summary then:

A) The right and left leg actions cancel each other out, with the hips rotating to act as mediator (Steps 1, 2, and 3).

B) The right arm and right shoulder cancel each other out, with the torso flexing to act as mediator (Steps 4, 5, and 6).

C) The left arm is free to act as a "wild card," to complete the balance of the muscular effort.

The end result of this coordinated movement is that your entire body, with all the strength you can muster, has delivered your right fist to the surface of your target, your partner's stomach, with an actual force insufficient to knock over a house of cards.

You will have to discover, or rediscover, how your own body actually works. You will have to learn consciously to isolate distinct sets of muscles. You will have to practice this isometric technique many times before you are comfortable with it or have confidence in it.

Figure 10 *Righthand body blow*

It is, however, relatively easy to learn, and very effective.

Obviously, the person receiving the blow has to maintain his part of the illusion, too. A normal person receiving a hard blow to the stomach will double over in pain. For one thing, he has been driven backward by the force of the blow. There will be a grunt, a rapid expulsion of breath, or some other vocal reaction that provides the audience with auditory proof that a real blow has landed. Here we have a matter of timing and coordination between the partners.

As the fist reaches the victim's stomach, the victim doubles over it. His torso moves backward 10 to 12 inches. This provides both dramatic reaction and a margin of safety in case the blow has not been completely "zeroed out." The recipient simply "retreats" with it and completes the reduction of the blow's force to zero, or at least to minimal propor-

tions. The assailant allows his fist to continue forward by remaining in contact with the shirt, or skin, of the victim. The assailant does not push any more than he actually punched the victim. The victim must not be knocked off balance. He must provide his own momentum for the reaction to the blow, just as, for the same reasons, he must provide his own momentum for a fall. Once the "blow" has landed (with zero foot-pounds of impact), the assailant maintains contact with the victim so that the illusion is sustained, but the victim provides and controls his own reaction. Because his body folds over and moves away from the fist as it arrives, the victim has maximum control of the situation and can provide the extra margin of safety for himself to make this kind of stage violence almost foolproof in terms both of illusion and of safety.

USE OF THE OTHER PARTS OF THE BODY TO DELIVER BLOWS

Delivering a blow with the other fist, with the knees, feet, or elbows, butting with the head or "blocking" with the torso, all follow the exact same principles and procedures. There are so many variables of height, weight, angle of attack, origin of attack (the part of the assailant's body), and point of attack (the target on the victim's body), that it is impossible to list the steps for each possibility. The principles inherent in the seven steps listed above will apply to virtually every situation you can construct for the stage. You must find the specific use of your musculature for the given body blow. Then divide your musculature's functions into opposing camps to provide for the isometric cancelation of actual foot-pounds of impact, and then practice it again and again, slowly, until you have the move and your partner's reaction to it firmly under control.

For example, if you are attacking with a foot or knee, then one foot is off the ground, and the two legs cannot cancel each other out. What do you do? Look at your body!

Step 1) When attacking with the right leg, either the knee or foot, the left leg is striding forward and is planted at a 45-degree angle, for balance. The left knee is flexed. The right leg is the attack weapon. Therefore, as soon as the left leg is planted it becomes the support of the whole body and can provide only minimum thrust, or the assailant will pitch himself off-balance. The calf and thigh muscles of the left leg are used in opposition, canceling out each other's thrust and stabilizing the assailant's balance.

Step 2a) If the weapon is your right knee, the thigh muscles are needed to bring the knee up into the victim. Use the calf muscles to isometrically balance out the thigh muscles. If your calf muscles aren't strong enough to

Figure 11 *Right knee to body*

balance the thigh muscles by themselves, then add in balance from the pelvic joints and hip muscles to "zero out" the thigh's thrust.

Step 2b) If the weapon is your right foot, then the calf muscles are thrusting the foot upward along with the front thigh muscles. Use the back thigh muscles, plus the knee joints and the pelvic action (distance control) to balance and cancel out the "throwing" muscles. Strike the victim with the sole of the foot, not the point of the toe.

Step 3) For both knee and foot attack, the hips retain their function of rotation for balance, and of mediation between the two isometrically balanced sets of leg muscles. Much more of the hip function is balance than it is mediation in this case, however, because you are on a one-point stance, not a two-point stance as in the case of a punch being thrown.

An attack with the knee must be carefully measured for distance and angle of attack. These factors will be determined by the relative height of the two performers, and their body configuration (two men 6 feet tall may have their waists at different heights because of differing torso and leg lengths). If they are too close and/or the angle is too shallow, the knee will wind up in the recipient's groin instead of his stomach. Further, as the distance traveled before contact is made will be shorter than anticipated in the planning of the move, the "braking action" will not yet be complete. The result of this kind of error can be extremely painful, although usually not lethal to this or succeeding generations.

An attack with the foot has the same requirements of distance and angle measurement. A further precaution, noted above in Step 2b, is that you ought to "strike" the victim with the sole of your foot, not the point of your toe. The reason for this is the greater amount of power generated by the leg muscles, an amount far in excess of that generated by the arm and fist. The sole of your foot, a broad, flat surface, is easier to absorb in the victim's torso, in case of error, than is the sharp point of your toe.

In addition, a punch affords the assailant two-point balance, as both his feet are on the ground. A kick requires one-point balance, as the second foot is traveling through the air to deliver the blow. This combination of greater potential velocity and lesser potential balance makes the kick a more dangerous move than its arm-delivered counterparts. The use of the flat sole of the foot, instead of the pointed toe, provides a greater and compensating margin for error.

In dealing with an elbow blow, remember that the victim is usually to the rear of the assailant. This type of blow is almost never used offensively. It is a defensive means of warding off attack. The person on the receiving end of this exchange is usually moving toward (or standing immediately behind) the assailant.

Step 1) With this movement, the right forearm and elbow are thrown into the victim and the shoulder is the main "brake."

Step 2) The bicep acts as "mediator."

Step 3) The left leg is forward, with the ball of the foot dug into the floor, thrusting backwards so the body will support the blow.

Step 4) The right leg is slightly to the rear and seems to be thrusting backward off the ball of the foot, in support of the blow. Actually you come right down on your heel and dig in as a brake.

Step 5) The hips swivel forward and to the left in "backswing preparation" for the blow, and then pivot rapidly backward. The illusion is one of support for the blow. In reality, the hips are simply taking up slack, balancing and canceling the action of your two legs against each other (net result: Zero pounds of thrust into the victim's body from the lower half of the assailant's body).

Step 6) The torso and left shoulder swivel with the right arm. Their main thrust is circular and forward, helping to cancel the thrust of the right elbow into the stomach of the victim.

In butting, blocking, and tackling, the principle is always the same. The torso and head go where the legs take them, so it is the legs and hips that control the move.

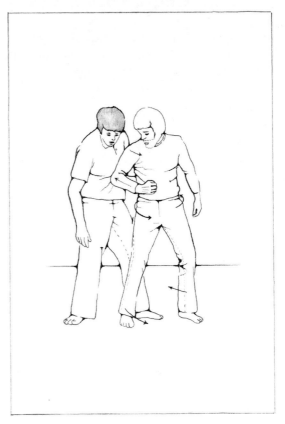

Figure 12 *Right elbow to body*

Step 1) The leg that is to the rear is planted and thrusting forward.

Step 2) The ball of the foot that is advanced is dug firmly into the floor and is braking.

Step 3) The hips swivel to take up the slack. All thrust is zeroed out.

Step 4) The head, or shoulder, is planted in the victim's stomach. The arms may be held back for balance, or they may be wrapped around the victim's torso.

Step 5) The victim then takes himself over and/or backward in reaction to the blow.

Step 6) The assailant, having made contact, simply follows the lead of the victim's reacting movement and maintains contact until the move is complete.

SUMMARY

In all of these body blows, regardless of how they are delivered, certain things remain constant:

1) The physical relationship of the two participants must be carefully planned, firmly set, and remain constant. Adjust it as often as necessary to make it comfortable and workable, but then *set it* and do not let it vary.

2) The same holds true for the angle and arc of the blow. Adjust it as often as necessary to get it right, then set it and do not let it vary.

3) Practice at half speed until kinesthetically secure (30 to 50 times, if necessary).

4) Practice at three-quarter speed until kinesthetically secure (30 to 50 times, if necessary).

5) Practice at full speed out of the context of the scene until kinesthetically secure. Only then can you incorporate the blow into the scene. (In Chapter XII we shall discuss the techniques of stringing together a series of blows into a choreographed fight.)

Note: If the blow in question leads to a fall, then you must follow the safety procedure noted in Chapter II of rehearsing on a mat until kinesthetically secure and then transferring practice to the hard stage floor. Do not shortcut this process! That's how people get hurt.

Chapter IV

HEAD BLOWS, UNARMED

In Chapter III I referred to the classic John Wayne movies in which he shook off the effect of being hit in the stomach with a 2″ x 4.″ One of my other favorite moments in "action drama" has occurred quite regularly in the television series *Gunsmoke*. This program has run for over more than two decades, and reruns have been and will be with us for decades more, providing excellent examples of illusory violence.

James Arness, who plays Marshal Dillon, is about 6 feet 6 inches tall and weighs roughly 240 pounds. For a long time, actors such as Chuck Connors and Charles Bronson made their living by being large enough to play villains opposite Arness. They were big enough to be able to fight with him without the visual aspect being either unsportsmanlike or ridiculous. In program after program, 500 pounds of well-tempered beef would square off; they would wind up from their heels, and smack each other full in the face. Despite their size and the backswing they took in preparation, it seemed that no fight ever ended with one blow. No, these men would flail away at each other with fists, boots, chairs, and pickax handles for three to five minutes before the villain finally bit the dust. Compare this to the real-life fact of Joe Louis, Rocky Marciano, Muhammad Ali, and Joe Frazier, all of whom ended fights against superbly conditioned and professional opponents with one or two blows to the head that traveled around *6 inches!* (And remember that they were wearing boxing gloves.)

What would really happen if all 240 pounds of Jim Arness were put behind a righthand punch that landed on an opponent's jaw? Well, for starters, every bone in Arness' right hand would probably be broken. Look at your own hand. Open the hand and look at the bones on the back of it. They are relatively fragile. Even balled into a fist, they are fragile. If you bounce them off someone's skull at even slightly the wrong angle, you are both going to need an orthopedic specialist!

What about the victim? Well, if the blow from a right cross lands full on his jaw, that section of his jaw is located somewhere in the middle of his mouth! Don't laugh, it isn't funny. The jawbone was not meant to take that kind of punishment. It will fracture, splinter, or separate completely when struck that hard. If the blow lands higher, on the cheek, then the cheekbone is shattered, the eye socket may be severely damaged, and because we don't know where all the bone splinters went, we don't know the condition of the eye itself. If the blow lands full-face, on the nose, we have several possibilities. The nose itself is surely broken, but the angle at which it was struck and the point at which it was broken are crucial. You see, the septum (the bone that supports the flesh of your nose) is a 2- to 3-inch needle-shaped bone, connected very tenuously to the skull, between the eyes. Immediately behind the septum is a hole, and immediately behind the hole is the brain. If the blow struck the nose at just the right angle, or if the septum's bridge to the skull had been snapped by an earlier blow, then the punch in question would drive 3 inches of sharp-pointed bone straight into the brain, killing the victim. If you think that is fantasy, ask a friend who has had Marine, Paratroop, Commando, or Special Forces training. They teach you how to do that on purpose in the "hand-to-hand" course. I must assume you would never do any of these things deliberately. However, they can all too easily happen by accident if you are careless, sloppy in your planning and preparation, or just "horsing around." Head blows are dangerous. Never play with them.

THE THEORY OF DELIVERING HEAD BLOWS

Blows to the head require great care. Isometric theory cannot be as safely and successfully employed here as with body blows, although it does play a part. The head does not bend and flex, as does the torso, to absorb the blow, and so a vital "margin for error" has been removed from the process. If a blow to the body is accidentally delivered too hard, the victim can simply ride backward with it, as he is already doubling over. This gives the assailant an extra fraction of a second to complete the braking action. If a blow to the head is too hard, and if it actually lands on the jaw, or elsewhere, there is no way the blow can be absorbed without pain and possible damage. Therefore, do not plan head blows to land; plan them to miss, and to create the illusion of contact.

PUNCHES TO THE HEAD

In delivering a punch to the victim's head, the assailant's job is essentially the same as for the body blow. He is still using his whole body, under isometric control. However, the blow is designed not to strike the face, but to miss by about one inch. Also, the blow does not stop in midair, at the point where it would have made contact with the victim's jaw or skull.

Step 1) Design the blow to come *across* the victim's head at a sharp angle, rather than directly into the victim's face or head.

Step 2) Plan to follow through on the blow as though it had landed and snapped the victim's head back.

Step 3) Design the arc of the blow to pass within an inch of the victim's face (preferably the point of his jaw) so that he will not be struck, even if he does not move.

Step 4) In proscenium always try to plan the punch so that it goes from downstage to upstage. This will give you a little more protection of illusion with a nervous or inexperienced cast that might make the margin much wider than the one inch requested in Step 3. However, provided you bring your fist across in front of the victim's face with the desired margin, the direction of delivery will make no difference. I have utilized this technique in arena production, within 2 feet of an audience, and they were positive the victim had been struck.

The victim is supposed to move, to react as if he has been struck. However, this way, the victim is safe from injury should he be either forgetful or late in his reaction.

The victim's job is also essentially the same as with a body blow. He must coordinate action and timing with the assailant so that he can react as though struck with the full force of the blow, while actually providing his own momentum. In dealing with head blows the victim's timing must be very sharp. He must snap his head back, out of the way of the blow, at the split second it arrives. If his timing is right, the audience cannot tell that the blow missed its target. His head and body movement must be in a direction, and of a size, consistent with the direction and force of the blow he has received. Timing is all: if the

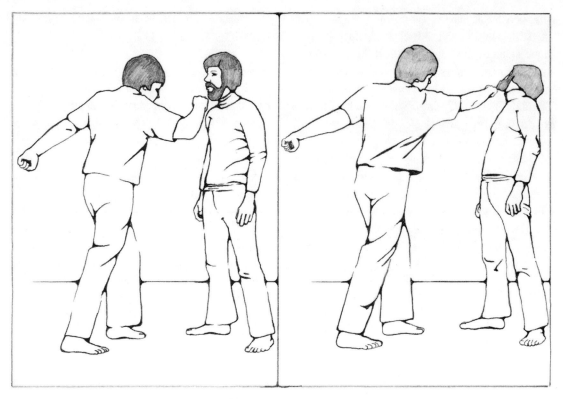

Figure 13 *Head blow*

victim is early or late, the whole business will look ridiculous. However, the assailant must plan the arc of his blow to miss the victim, even at the risk of the moment's "not working," of its "looking ridiculous." A ridiculous moment in the play, even one that "ruins" the evening, is always preferable to the hospitalization of a performer.

There is a temptation to try to avoid the risk of missing too wide by aiming the arc of the blow to come through the space vacated by the victim's jaw as he snaps his head back. This will work fine if the timing is perfect. It will look just as bad as the arc that goes by one inch in front of the face if the victim snaps back too early (something he is more likely to do if he knows that fist is really coming at him). It is an idea that can have tragic consequences if the victim snaps his head back too late. He will be struck full on the face by the blow. The risk is not worth it; always plan the arc to miss.

As the blow is "struck" the victim will, again, provide some vocal sound (a gasp, groan, or cry) to cover the fact that there is no sound of fist on bone.

This kind of business requires the same care and precision of preparation as laid out in the summary of Chapter III on body blows. Set your space relationship, foot placement, and the arc of the blow very carefully. Practice it many times at half speed, then three-quarter speed until it is kinesthetically secure, and practice it out of context until you have it down pat. Only then can you put it in a scene.

USE OF OTHER PARTS OF THE BODY

The basic instructions for landing and receiving punches also apply when the victim is being "struck" with the assailant's knee, foot, or elbow. Again, the assailant is under good isometric control, but he must bring the "weapon" through and finish the move. It must not stop at the "point of contact." It must go past the victim's head, not into it or through the vacated space. Because of the difficulty of "masking," I do not recommend the use of feet or knees in an arena situation. A well-coordinated and experienced pair of actors can make the technique work, but if your audience can see the action clearly and close up, you will have to shave either your dramatic or your safety margin for error too closely to assure the success of the illusion. Settle for the use of the fist. It is tremendously effective when done close to an audience. In proscenium, always plan for the knee, foot, or elbow to travel from downstage to upstage as it arcs across the victim's head.

SUMMARY

See the summary page of Chapter III on body blows, and apply it. It is identical to the needs of this chapter. In addition, remember that these blows are likely to lead to a high-velocity fall on the part of the victim. If the victim is to slump or be driven to the ground, the assailant is to deliver only the pretext for the fall, not the actual impetus. Let the victim blend his reaction to the head blow into his fall on his own, providing his own impetus and his own momentum.

Chapter V

WRESTLING AND UNARMED MARTIAL ARTS

A great ethos and mythos have grown up around the martial arts in the late 1960's and early 1970's. They have been glorified and painstakingly demonstrated on television, film, and stage. James Bond, in particular, has used these techniques in a steady stream of action films. So have *Our Man Flint, The Manchurian Candidate,* and an endless list of war heroes, war villains, police and detective characters, and their nemeses. Various and sundry psychotics and ascetics (such as Cain in the series *Kung Fu*) have demonstrated the ease with which one can dispatch an opponent. Probably the greatest martial-arts entertainment hero of the early 1970's was Bruce Lee, who made a long and profitable series of *Kung Fu* films in which he demonstrated his ability to maim and defeat scores of opponents at one time. There is only one problem with Bruce Lee. He's dead!

On July 20, 1973, Bruce Lee collapsed and died. A coroner's inquest was held in Hong Kong, and on September 18, 1973, the Associated Press reported that the inquest had found a substantial relationship between the death and "several very hard blows to the head during filming of Chinese fighting scenes in the months before his death."

Before going into martial arts, however, let us look at the more fundamental aspects of wrestling for the stage. These concepts are simpler and less flashy, but they are more commonly used.

Theory of Wrestling for the Stage

When we speak of "wrestling" for the theatre, we are not dealing with either the staged version of the professional wrestling match, or with the real athletic competition of high school, N.C.A.A., or Olympic wrestling. In each of these cases, the two men involved are *competing.* They are working against each other, each seeking a victory, and their full strength is engaged, each in opposition to the other, each seeking an advantage to throw the other off balance. On the stage, the two actors must be working in cooperation with each other, striving to create the illusion of force and counterforce while actually leaving each other free to fall or tumble at will, on cue, each one secure in the full possession of his own balance. Isometrics is employed to create the illusion of force on the part of the assailant, while in reality zero pounds of thrust are in effect. The victim uses isometrics to "resist." The assailant thus provides motivation for the victim to fling himself around, or down onto, the stage. The same is true of "martial arts." Judo throws (which are, in many instances, similar to wrestling throws) and karate blows are all illusory rather than real, with isometrics being the basis of the illusion. There is an added procedure by which the assailant can assist and protect the victim during a throw; this will be described in detail later in this chapter.

Application and Use in Stage Wrestling

Formal wrestling matches are very rare in dramatic literature. Orlando and Charles have a "match" in Act I, Scene iii of Shakespeare's *As You Like It,* but I am hard pressed to think of many more examples. Actually, most "wrestling" in plays (and "on the street") consists of grappling, hauling, and pulling, with each of the combatants grabbing for a "target of opportunity" in the area of the shoulders, waist, or legs. In almost all dramatic cases, we are really dealing with "street fighting," not wrestling.

Stage wrestling is all isometrics. A summary of the principles set forth in Chapter III on body blows applies here as well:

1) Any move, and countermove, can be divided into its component parts.

2) The muscular action of each part can be determined.

3) The muscles in that action can be set in isometric opposition.

In real wrestling the goal is to throw and pin your opponent to the ground. In stage wrestling, the goal is to *assist* your partner as he takes himself down. A forward arm-throw, for example, does not consist of a minimally controlled crash. It consists instead of: a) a self-initiated forward somersault on the part of the victim, which is b) given pretext and then assisted by the assailant. All the assailant has to do is reverse his normal muscle thrust. Instead of throwing his victim to the ground, he is giving support and motivation for the victim on the way down. If done quickly and smoothly, it looks the same as a really violent "throw," but the victim has maintained control all the way.

One of the most common movements in both wrestling and "unorganized grappling" comes when the two men have grabbed each other by the arms or shoulders and are trying to pull each other off balance. In normal wrestling, each is using all the strength in his body, legs, and both arms to yank the opponent over to the right or left. On stage, try pressing inward with both hands, as though trying to telescope the shoulders of your partner together. You cannot actually do that, of course, but in attempting to do it you are isometrically can-

Figure 14 *Isometric grappling in wrestling*

celing out all of your effort, and allowing your partner to keep his balance and be master of his own movement.

As above, recognize that when this action leads to a fall (as opposed to a wrestling throw, which requires two-man cooperation), the victim must provide his own impetus and momentum. Wrestling on the stage can be effective and a lot of fun. It has a tendency, however, to be less clearly planned and less crisp in execution than specific head and body blows. This is incorrect and unsafe. Wrestling sequences require the same care and choreograhpy as anything else. Plan them out step by step.

Judo and Wrestling Throws

The basic safety technique involved in using any kind of "throw" for the stage involves the placement of the assailant's feet and center of balance. When you are actually trying to hurt someone, you attempt to get his feet out from under him. Essentially, you are trying to get him off his center of balance. Once this is accomplished, you get your own body out of the way and let him crash to the floor. For stage purposes:

1) You still try to destroy your "opponent's" balance; that is, you isometrically create the illusion that you have done so, or that you have lifted your victim's feet from the floor.

2) *However,* instead of getting your body out of the way and allowing him to crash, you set your feet and weight in such a way that your "outboard" leg becomes a ramp for the victim to roll down. This way, there is no crash. The victim leaves his feet, rolls down your thigh and calf, and leaves the protection of your leg-ramp at about ankle height. That doesn't leave him very far to fall.

Backward hip-rolls

Step 1) The two partners start by facing each other, but not quite nose to nose. For a throw off of the right hip they should be offset with their right shoulders overlapping, instead. They should be no more than one stride away from each other as the sequence is about to begin. If they start toward each other from a greater distance, then take that into account in planning the choreography of the business.

Step 2) The assailant strides forward on his left foot. This stride should bring the heel of his left foot to a depth of 3 to 6 inches behind the heels of the victim, and very close to the victim's right foot.

Step 3a) The assailant swings his right leg past the body of the victim in a J-shaped motion that brings his foot to rest behind the victim with his right hip planted in the small of the victim's back. The assailant must angle his right leg as wide as possible and plant his right foot as far outside of the victim's left leg as he can, while maintaining a solid balance of his own. This is the ramp the victim will slide down.

Step 3b) The victim, in order to assist the assailant in 3a, should sway and/or lean a little to the left, to allow easy passage of the assailant's body to the correct position. As the assailant's body goes past the victim, the victim sways and/or leans back into an upright, balanced position.

Step 4a) As the assailant strides into position 3a, his right arm will come through, parallel to the floor, in a scything motion. This motion must always be across the shoulders, never across the neck. Bringing your forearm across someone's neck is a dangerous move that can cause choking, muscle strains, or worse.

Step 4b) If you are the victim, give way before the arm. Do not wait to be forced back on your assailant's hip. Lean backward pivoting toward your left, and let your weight fall across the firmly planted right leg and hip of your assailant.

Step 5) As of step 3a, the assailant had both legs firmly planted, and he is in a good position to support weight. The victim's full weight now falls upon the assailant. The jointure of the two bodies should be at the pelvis. This is the fulcrum of balance. If the victim's left hip (at the side of the hip) strikes the assailant's right hip at the top of the ramp-leg, then the two bodies should be comfortably balanced.

Step 6a) The assailant's right arm has continued through the scything motion and is still wrapped around the victim's shoulders, with the right hand gripping the victim's left shoulder. This allows the assailant's arm to act as a brake and as a balance. Because of this, at this split second, there should be no danger of the victim falling off of his supporting ramp-leg. As the victim begins his roll down the ramp, let go.

Step 6b) Simultaneously, the victim tucks

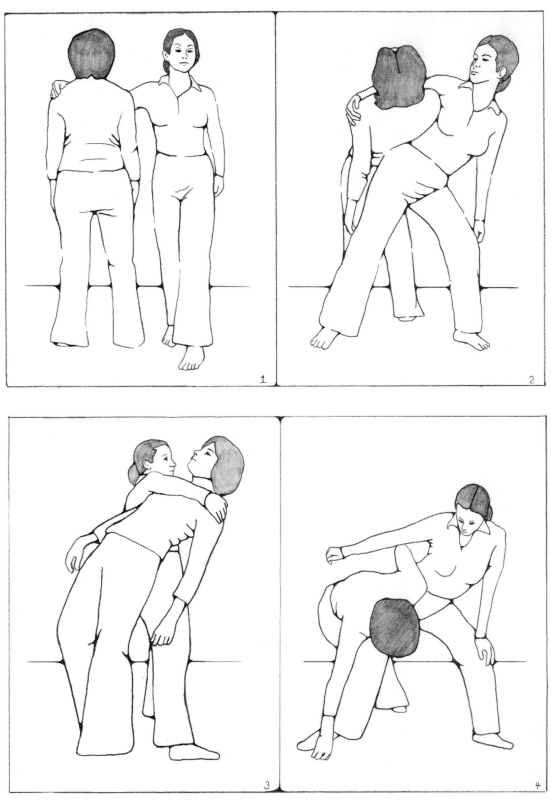

Figures 15 and 16   *Backward hip-roll*

his arms into his chest, and rolls down the ramp-leg onto the floor. The victim should not leave the protection of the ramp until he is at approximately ankle level. This means a "crash" to the floor from a final height of 4 inches.

Step 7a) After the victim has left the ramp-leg, the assailant pivots away from his supporting posture and moves into position for the next piece of business.

Step 7b) Upon leaving the ramp and reaching the floor, the victim "rolls out" the momentum of the business, according to the motivation given him (e.g., how hard was he theoretically "thrown"?).

Notes: 1) The victim must provide his own momentum to *roll* down the ramp-leg, instead of *sliding* down out of control. To do this, Steps 4b through 6b must be accomplished in a continuous motion, and the victim must impel himself into this sequence with enough force to achieve a rolling motion down the leg-ramp. If the victim places himself delicately on the assailant's hip, there will be no momentum, and he will slide unceremoniously to the floor with a thump. He will still have the ramp; it will still not be a real crash. However, it will be neither as dramatically effective nor as comfortable as a rolling motion.

2) To achieve a left-side hip-roll, reverse the assignment of foot placement, and follow the same instructions.

3) Always practice this on a mat until you are absolutely sure of it. Kinesthetic security is vital to both the emotional and physical security of the actor being thrown.

Forward hip-rolls

Step 1) The two partners start by facing each other. The situation is identical to Step 1 in the backward hip-roll, except that their left shoulders are offset instead of their right shoulders.

Step 2) The assailant strides into the victim on his left leg. He plants the leg and pivots on the ball of his left foot, turning inside of and across in front of the body of the victim. When the left leg first hits the ground, the toe is pointed toward the victim and the foot is placed midway between the victim's feet. When the pivot on the ball of the left foot is complete, the toe of the left foot is pointed away from the victim.

Step 3a) The assailant's right leg comes around, inside of the victim's body, and is planted as far outside of the victim's right leg as can be managed, while maintaining a solid balance of his own. Here is the leg-ramp again.

Step 3b) The assailant's right arm swings up, during 3a, and hooks under the left arm of the victim. The jointure here should be at the shoulder, with the bicep of the assailant's right arm jamming into the left armpit of the victim. The assailant carries the motion through and "forces" the victim onto his hip.

Step 4) 3a and 3b happen almost simultaneously (actually 3b trails 3a by part of a second or so). This means that the victim is already starting to be "lifted off his feet" in Step 3. Actually, as soon as the victim starts to feel the pressure of 3b, he tucks his right arm into his chest and starts to throw himself forward onto the leg-ramp of the assailant.

Step 5a) The assailant has planted the leg-ramp as firmly as possible. His right arm sweeps through the move, still wrapped around the victim's torso, as a safety precaution. He should be sure, however, that he has released the victim's left arm, so the victim may tuck it in for the roll down the ramp.

Step 5b) The victim brings himself in to the top of the ramp-leg with sufficient momentum to roll down the ramp. This means that the victim is rotating toward his *left,* into the assailant's body. The victim must remember to tuck his left arm into his chest as soon as it is disengaged from the assailant in Steps 3b to 5a. The jointure of the two bodies should be at the pelvis, just as in the back hip-throw. The victim's pelvic bone should strike

Figures 17, 18, 19, and 20 *Forward hip-roll*

the assailant's leg-ramp right at the side of the hip. With this balanced jointure, and with the assailant's right arm still in contact with the victim's torso for additional balance, there should be no danger of falling off the ramp.

Step 6) The victim rolls down the ramp, onto the floor, leaving the ramp at approximately ankle height.

Step 7a) After the victim has left the ramp-leg, the assailant pivots away from his supporting position and moves into position for the next piece of business.

Step 7b) Upon leaving the ramp and reaching the floor, the victim "rolls out" the momentum of the business, according to the motivation given him (e.g., how hard was he theoretically "thrown"?).

Notes: All three notes on the section on Backward Hip-rolls apply to Forward Hip-rolls as well.

Summary

In dealing with both forward and backward hip-rolls, please recognize that in setting the angle of the ramp and of the two bodies, I was working on the premise of two persons of approximately the same size. This is a premise that does not always hold true. Not only do men and women vary greatly in size, weight, and configuration within their own sex, but you may have a situation in which you wish a girl to "throw" a man much larger than herself. Therefore please note the following:

(1) The key point is always to have a hip-to-hip jointure at the top of the ramp. With two people of roughly the same size, when the assailant's ramp-leg is set, the assailant's body is usually parallel to the body of the victim. This is at the moment before the victim leaves his feet to fall onto the ramp. The angle between the two bodies is zero degrees.

If the assailant and victim are of significantly different heights, then you have to adjust the relative position and angle of the two

bodies at this moment, so that when the victim falls onto the assailant's leg-ramp the victim's hip lands on the assailant's hip. For example, if the assailant is 5′8″ and the victim is 6′2″, this may involve the assailant's planting his right foot in such a way that there is an angle of 30 degrees between the two bodies (or even 45 degrees). If "Stringbean" is being thrown by "Peanut", the assailant may have to pivot enough to achieve an angle of up to 90 degrees, so that instead of being back to back (on a back hip-roll), the assailant pivots and plants his right foot at a point where his left shoulder and side are facing the victim's back. The angle between the two bodies can vary from 0 degrees to 90 degrees and the move will still work as long as the jointure at the top of the ramp is hip to hip.

Of course, as the angle between the bodies increases, the move becomes more difficult for the victim. This is because of Steps 4a and 4b on the backward hip-roll and Step 4 on the forward hip-roll. In both cases, the assailant's arm is scything through the torso of the victim as the assailant plants his right foot to establish the ramp. This means that the victim has to move with the arm and start his fall onto the ramp. The wider the angle between the bodies, the longer it takes the assailant to establish the ramp, and the farther the victim has to fall before he makes contact with the ramp. There may well be a point of diminishing returns where the angle is just too wide and the timing just too tight for actors to be comfortable with this move. If you find this is the case, please forget the hip-roll at that point in the script, and use a different piece of business.

2) There is definitely and without question a point at which the disparity of size and weight makes the establishment of an adequate and safe leg-ramp impossible. Do not ask a 110-pound girl to establish a ramp for a 240-pound actor. She can't do it! When the disparity of size and weight between assailant and victim is too great, or when a correctly posi-

tioned ramp will still not sustain the victim's weight, both persons are likely to get hurt. The assailant's knee will be particularly vulnerable as the ramp she has established collapses. I am, however, talking about gross disparity. I weigh 180 pounds and have been "thrown" by a 110-pound girl quite satisfactorily.

3) These throws cannot be practiced in slow motion. They just won't work that way. They *can* be practiced in *stop-action* step by step:

a) Practice getting the leg positions right. Don't use the arms.

b) Add in the arm motions, but stop short of the victim's taking the roll down the ramp. At this point in the practice, have the assailant bend the victim back to the point of hip-to-hip contact on the top of the ramp and then hold on for dear life.

c) Then put it all together, including the roll down the ramp.

d) Always practice on a mat until you are kinesthetically secure in the move.

e) Always practice out of the context of the scene until you are kinesthetically secure in the move.

f) Practice on the hard floor of the stage, out of context, until you are secure, and then—only then—put it into the scene.

Forward arm-throws and arm-locks

Step 1) The two partners start by facing each other, but not quite nose to nose. For a throw based on the victim's right arm, the partners should be offset, with the right shoulders overlapping.

Step 2) The assailant strides forward on his left foot to close the distance, and grasps the victim's right arm, at and above the wrist, with both of his hands, using the same grip he would use on a baseball bat.

Step 3a) The assailant pivots in a 270-degree turn to his left, twisting the victim's

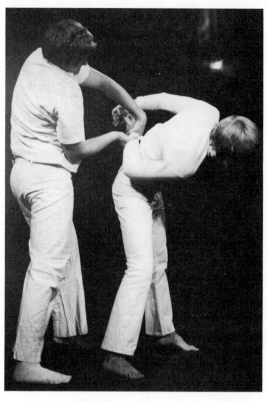

Figure 21 *Forward arm-throw or lock*

arm over his own head as he goes. Stop with the victim's arm twisted behind his back, but with no pressure on the joints.

Step 3b) The victim pivots 90 degrees to his left on the ball of his left foot. This will counter the pressure from the assailant's move to do just that. This is a regular judo move. The victim is either going to pivot 90 degrees left of his own volition and with his own balance, or he is going to be forced to that position by pressure on his wrist, elbow, and shoulder. When the assailant and victim do this move together, in a coordinated manner, there is no discomfort and no loss of balance.

Step 4a) For an *arm-lock,* the assailant isometrically pretends to force the arm upward to a pain-inducing position. The victim is the one who actually raises his own right arm as much as he can without hurting himself. The victim also reacts with his whole body, as though he were in as much pain as the performance situation calls for. From this

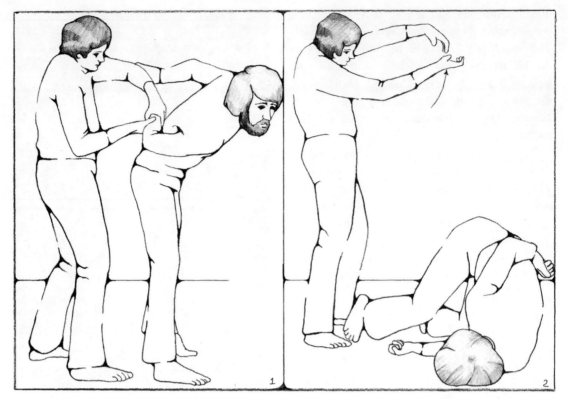

Figure 22   *Forward arm-throw, step 4b*

position the assailant can "freeze" the victim, or force him to his knees.

Step 4b) For a forward *arm-throw* the victim simply relaxes at the knees and goes into a forward somersault, which he "rolls out" to whatever extent is desired. The assailant simply allows the victim's right arm to travel upward, forward, and out of his hands as the victim somersaults forward. The assailant can give a little flourish of "momentum" by swinging his hands upward just after he lets go of the arm.

Note: If the victim is going to his knees, in Step 4a above, do not crash downward. The kneecap is vulnerable. Remember Chapter I:

Step 1) The center of weight and balance is the pelvis. Bring your pelvis forward directly over the balls of your feet.

Step 2) Bring your weight down and forward until your toes are gripping the floor for balance and you are just about sitting on your heels.

Step 3) Lean your weight forward on, and then over, your toes until you have *placed* your knees on the floor. Swaying your shoulders and head backward as you do this will provide compensatory balance and allow your torso to remain as upright as you wish it to be.

For a forward arm-lock or throw based on the victim's left hand, simply reverse the directions.

Rear arm-lock

Step 1) For a rear arm-lock the assailant approaches the victim from the rear, with his body slightly offset to the right of the victim's body.

Step 2) The assailant "yokes" the victim by encircling his neck and throat with the assailant's left arm. In this maneuver, the rear of the assailant's left forearm comes across the throat of the victim. Be careful not to put any pressure on the victim's throat.

Figure 23   *Rear arm-lock*

Step 3a) The assailant grasps the victim's right wrist with his own right hand and twists the victim's right arm up behind his back. This maneuver should not be forced.

Step 3b) The victim brings his own right arm up behind his back at the cue from the assailant. There should be no pressure from the assailant. As the victim, you are providing your own motion and momentum. Your right arm should go no further than you want it to.

Step 4) The assailant and victim isometrically create body tension and struggle commensurate with the situation. The victim reacts with appropriate pain-motivation. Both have maintained their balance.

Backward arm-throw (off of a hip-roll, or as a leg-drop)

This is actually a variant either of the backward hip-roll or of the backward leg-drop, which will be described in the next section.

Step 1) The assailant and victim face each other, but offset, to the right, shoulder to shoulder.

Step 2) The assailant steps in with his left foot to close the distance.

Step 3) The assailant and victim hook, or link, right arms at the elbow joint.

Step 4a) (off the hip-roll) The assailant pivots toward the left on the balls of both feet, while sliding his right leg outward as far as possible to establish the leg ramp.

Step 4b) (as a leg-drop) The assailant sweeps his right foot in a rearward scything motion that catches the victim about ankle-high at the rear of his right leg. The victim brings his own right foot up and forward in response to this cue.

Step 5a) The assailant and victim now complete Steps 5 through 7 of the backward hip-roll, as the victim rolls down the leg-ramp. Instead of the assailant's arm around the victim's torso being the brake, however,

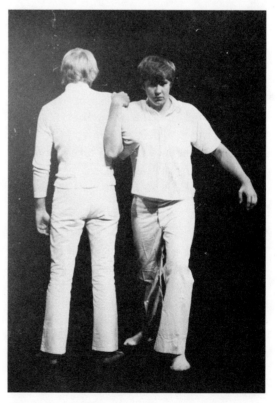

Figure 24   *Backward arm-throw, Steps 1, 2, and 3*

Figure 25   *Backward arm-throw off a hip-roll, Step 4a*

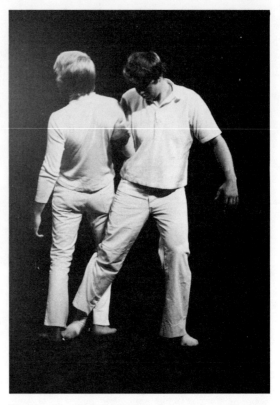

Figure 26   *Backward arm-throw off a leg-drop, Step 4b*

the linked elbows provide the brake. Otherwise the completion is the same.

Step 5b) The victim's right leg has now come out from under him. He may do either a left side-fall or a sit-down back-fall (See Chapter I) to complete the move.

Note: The same move can be taken from the left by reversing the instructions.

LEG-DROPS

Forward leg-drop

Step 1) The assailant and victim face each other, offset shoulder to shoulder.

Step 2) The assailant strides into the victim on the leg farthest from the victim, to close the distance between them.

Step 3a) The assailant trails in with the foot nearest the victim and hooks the top of that foot (not the toe or side of the shoe) into the shin of the victim's near-side leg, "forcing" it backward.

Step 3b) At the same time, the assailant places the palm of his near-side hand on the top or rear of the victim's near-side shoulder and "pushes" the victim's torso forward.

(In neither Step 3a nor Step 3b is pressure truly applied; the assailant is merely cueing the victim.)

Step 4) As the victim receives the cues from Steps 3a and 3b, he initiates a forward somersault, or a side-fall to the side being swept out from under him. In either case, the victim retains his balance and initiates his own fall, on cue. The assailant must not force him down.

Backward leg-drop

Step 1) The assailant may approach the victim from the front, side, or rear. From whichever direction, the final stride should bring the assailant to one side of the victim and parallel to him.

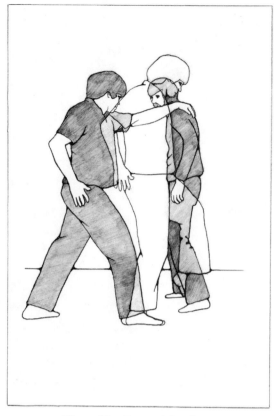

Figure 27 *Forward leg-drop*

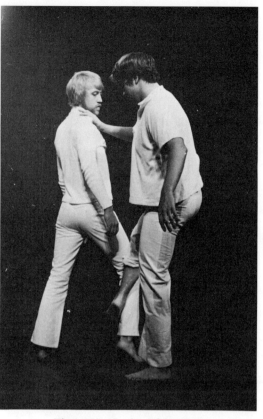

Figure 28 *Backward leg-drop*

Step 2a) The assailant puts all his weight on the foot farthest from the victim. He brings the other foot into position and hooks the *top* of his foot into the Achilles' tendon of the victim, about ankle-high, on the leg of the victim closest to him. The direction and pressure of this move is from the rear toward the front of the victim, "forcing" his foot forward.

Step 2b) At the same time the assailant uses his hand nearest the victim's near shoulder. He slaps that hand, palm first, into the front of the victim's shoulder, "pushing" the victim's torso backward. (Remember that Steps 2a and 2b must be isometrically neutral. They are cues only.)

Step 3) As the victim receives the cues from Steps 2a and 2b, he initiates either a back-fall off of a side-fall toward the leg being swept out from under him, or a sit-down back-fall. In either case, the victim retains his balance and initiates his own fall, on cue.

Defensive leg-drop

This move is used as a defensive maneuver, when the assailant is flat on his back and the victim is moving toward him to attack.

Step 1) The victim strides in to the assailant, closing the distance between them. When he stops, that is, when he reaches the point of contact, all of his weight should be on the forward leg.

Step 2a) When the victim has reached the point of contact, the assailant hooks one leg around the Achilles' tendon at the rear of the victim's forward leg. Be sure your contact is the top of your foot against the tendon, about ankle-high.

Step 2b) As soon as Step 2a is complete, and all but simultaneous with it, place the sole of your other foot against the thigh of the

Figure 29 *Defensive leg-drop*

victim's forward foot. Be sure that your foot is angled across the thigh, not parallel to it, and is placed safely above the victim's knee. (Note that the assailant's upper foot in Figure 29 is *not* placed correctly across the victim's thigh.) He will need to flex his knee to complete his move and if your foot is against the knee you will hamper his balance. Also, the kneecap is highly vulnerable to bruising. (Steps 2a and 2b together provide the illusion of a scissors action. Do not actually apply pressure with either foot, or you will lift your partner right off his feet and hurt him. These actions are cues only.)

Step 3) As the victim receives the cues from Steps 2a and 2b, he will dig the ball and toes of his front foot into the ground as a brake, and thrust himself backward onto his rear foot. The victim then continues the motion into a sit-down back-fall.

Summary

Unlike hip-rolls, these moves do lend themselves to slow-motion practice, up to the point where the victim initiates the fall. You can find your angle and placement of attack while moving in slow motion and thus ensure both accuracy and safety. Practice these moves sequentially, going in slow motion and in stop-action, one step at a time, right up to the point of the fall, which the victim will take at full speed to maintain body control. Practice on a mat first, then on the stage floor. Be sure you are kinesthetically secure at each stage before going on to the next.

Weapon disarms

Weapon disarms are all variants of the judo-wrestling techniques noted in Chapter

V. It does not matter whether the weapon is a gun, knife, sword, club, baseball bat, or lead pipe. The point is that the weapon carrier has it in one or both of his hands.

If the weapon is in one hand and static, then the idea is to get inside of the weapon and grasp the wrist and/or arm of the hand holding it. After that you just proceed with the hip-roll, arm-throw, or leg-drop of your choice. There are certain additional rules to remember:

If the weapon either is, or is being used as, a blunt instrument and it is being swung at you, then:

a) The weapon carrier must swing the weapon in a wide arc to allow the disarmer to get inside of that arc and block the blow. This is *not* a contest; it is a choreographed piece of business.

b) The disarmer steps inside the arc of the blow and blocks it by coming across the forearm of the weapon carrier, with his own near-side forearm. The two forearms should meet at right angles, in the middle of both forearms. That will give you both maximum target area and maximum margin for error.

c) Once the weapon blow has been blocked and the forearms are in solid contact, you are ready to proceed with the hip-roll, arm-throw, or leg-drop of your choice.

If the weapon carrier is to fall to the ground, then he must get rid of the weapon before he starts his fall, so that there is no danger of his falling on it. Before leaving his feet the weapon carrier lets go of the weapon, making sure that it travels a) away from himself and his partner; b) upstage, away from the audience; c) in a line of direction clear of any other actors; and d) in a line of direction that will not take it through a piece of scenery.

Obviously, the actor and director must plan the "flight-line" of the weapon carefully as part of the choreography of the fight.

Weapon exchanges

A weapon that is held in both hands, such as a pool cue, quarterstaff, spear, or rifle, also lends itself to the following:

Step 1) The weapon carrier grasps the weapon firmly in both hands, spread wide on the weapon, as he and the disarmer close in on each other. He holds it, or at the last moment turns it, so that the weapon is parallel to his body.

Step 2) The disarmer grasps the weapon with both hands *inside* the hands of the weapon carrier.

Step 3a) The disarmer puts all his weight on his left foot and steps back with his right foot, moving into a sit-down back-fall.

Step 3b) At the same time, the weapon carrier shifts towards his right so as to give clearance to the disarmer's body and starts forward into a somersault. (Both men are still holding onto the weapon.)

Step 4a) As soon as the disarmer gets his buttocks on the floor, he places his left foot into the abdomen of the weapon carrier and *assists* him over into the somersault. This is a supporting move, not a kick!

Step 4b) As soon as he feels that foot supporting, the weapon carrier lets go of the weapon and completes his forward somersault.

Step 5) The weapon carrier "rolls out" his somersault and comes to his feet ready to continue, but disarmed. The disarmer now has the weapon! He can get to his feet and the fight can continue.

Any weapon that has been disarmed from and/or dropped by the weapon carrier can naturally be retrieved by the disarmer, thus completing an exchange.

A disarm and/or exchange can also be achieved by use of a karate chop upon the weapon-carrying arm or wrist. Just be sure, in such an event, that the two rules given in the Weapon disarms section above are followed. You simply substitute the karate chop for the "throw" or "drop" as the means of resolving the move.

KARATE AND JUDO BLOWS AND MARTIAL ARTS

What not to do and why

Everything described and demonstrated to this point is dangerous if done poorly or carelessly. It can result in great discomfort and/or injury. Karate, judo, and other martial-arts blows are more than dangerous. They are potentially lethal. There are, therefore, several things you should never attempt, however dramatically attractive they seem and however often you have seen professional stunt men and professionally trained stage combatants do them. Bruce Lee was as well trained as they come. Bruce Lee is dead.

The neck

First, stay away from the neck and throat. Judo and karate chops to the neck and throat area have almost no margin for error if your isometrics fail you and you are not "zeroed out" at the moment of contact. A blow delivered directly to the base of the neck will result in a nerve-pinch and a blackout on the part of the victim—just as in the movies. If you make an error of judgment, or if the victim moves his head 2 inches right or left, your blow will land in the gap between two vertebrae and your victim can wind up with a broken neck. If you "strike" the side of the neck, over the carotid artery, you will again have only a blackout to contend with. But if your victim turns his head toward you and you accidentally come across the Adam's apple, that cartilage will be crushed and the victim will suffocate.

Well, can't you use these movements at all? Of course you *can*. Proper use of isometric technique will allow you to "strike" a victim anywhere on his neck with the side of your hand, and actually "bounce off of" your target area with zero pounds of impact. However, the repercussions of error are so drastic, and the margin for error is so slight, that I urgently warn that you *should not*.

The torso

Side-of-the-hand chops, isometrically controlled, are fine for the front of the torso. There is a lot of resilience in the torso. There is the ability to "ride with" the blow. Most important, vital internal organs are protected by layers of muscle, fat, and bone. However, stay away from the kidney area, at the rear of the torso. Here the protective insulation is not so great, and the torso doesn't bend or "give" that way to take up the slack of an error in the velocity of the assailant's blow. An errant chop to the kidneys can cause real pain and/or damage.

A blow delivered with the tips of the five fingers, grouped close together to form a ridge, is another matter. You can isometrically throw that into the solar plexus (the pit of the stomach) and an error can be compensated for as the victim doubles over. In any event, the worst you can get is a very sore stomach and a momentary loss of consciousness. However, if the victim turns his body a bit in either direction—and if he is in normal (and by that I mean flabby) condition—you will drive an errant blow into his gallbladder or spleen, depending on which direction he turned. If he is like most of us, you run the risk of macerating the organ in question. A hand set in karate position will dig into the body in a manner totally unlike the balled fist. Do not underestimate the damage you can do. Never plan a karate or judo chop in the area of the gallbladder or spleen, and if you must plan one to land in the solar plexus, position it with extreme care.

The head

Stay away from the face and skull. Stay away from the skull for the sake of the assailant's hand, which is no match for that hard bone. You will create no illusion of damage done to the victim, and the assailant can really wrack up his hand. The face—nose and eyes—are terribly vulnerable. You have virtually no margin for error either in space relationships or in the velocity of the blow. Never plan *anything* of a martial-arts nature to land on the face.

What you can safely do, and how

First of all, in dealing with karate-judo and martial-arts blows, be aware that you are dealing entirely in isometrics. These blows, one and all, should land with a velocity measured in ounces, not pounds. Second, all blows are to be choreographed to "rebound off of" the target, not to "drive through" it. This assists in the isometric choreography, and provides an added margin of safety.

A) Having just told you not to plan neck blows, let me tell you how to do them safely, so that both the audience and you can be satisfied. There is no contradiction. The blows never land on the neck. Always assuming isometric control and a "rebound" flight-pattern for the blow, aim it for the shoulder of the victim roughly 3 inches from the jointure of neck and shoulder. The rebound arc of the blow and the flurry of large body activity will keep the audience from seeing where it really landed. A blow simulated to land on the base of the neck actually comes down on the victim's back, also 3 to 4 inches below the vital area. Same illusion. Same result. This is truly a matter of "the hand is quicker than the (audience's) eye." There is no safe way to go for the throat itself. Don't try it.

B) Karate-judo chops on the point of the shoulder (which would cause momentary nerve paralysis), the elbow, forearm, or wrist of the victim are excellent and flashy "disarming" techniques. They carry little risk so long as they are isometrically controlled, and so long as they are planned to bounce off of the target, not drive through it.

C) Almost all of the sections in this chapter—wrestling, hip-rolls, arm-throws, and weapon disarms and exchanges—lend themselves to and can be presented as martial arts. It depends on the style and crispness with which the moves are executed. Martial arts have often been referred to as "the scientific art of dirty fighting." The only difference between most of the above and "street-fighting" is the crisp style with which it is done. When Marlon Brando or Steve McQueen gives you an elbow, it is street-fighting. When Bruce Lee or David Carradine does the same thing, it is called karate, or Kung Fu.

D) Look at the materials in Chapters III and IV on using the elbows, knees, and feet against the head and body. If done with elegance and grace, these same pieces of business will transform themselves from "gutter tactics" to Oriental wisdom. The difference is a matter of style, not of technique.

This is, of course, a gross simplification. Training in the martial arts is a serious business. It takes years of study and is a matter of spiritual as well as physical involvement. However, we are not expecting the actor to give a long, sustained demonstration of one or more of these martial arts, and we are not expecting him to become a true master. We are trying to create an illusion of capability for a few seconds at a time. For this purpose, style, combined with the discipline of an actor who knows the inherent dangers of the business and treats it with proper respect, will do the job.

SPECIAL TECHNIQUES FOR WOMEN

The term "he" is used throughout this book for literary convenience, to avoid the awkward "he and/or she" construction. Women are as capable of learning, teaching, and performing these techniques as men are, and are in equal need of them.

In this particular short section, please allow me to turn the tables. The following segments on hair-pulling, scratching, and choking are perhaps used more often by female characters than by males, but they are equally applicable to men. They can be used on men. They can be used by men.

Hair-pulling

Hairstyles for both men and women have changed drastically during the 20th century. The changes have been frequent and unpredictable. So the first premise we must work with is that the character in question, male or female, will have enough hair to pull. A close-cropped hairstyle does not afford the assailant enough of a target, or enough of a grip.

On genuine historical battlefields, be they battles of individuals or of armies, hair has been a very real factor. The Roman soldier was clean-shaven by order of the battlefield strategist, who realized that a beard gave the enemy something to grab and throw his men off balance with. Soldiers wore their hair short, or under helmets, or braided and tucked, so that they would not present their enemies with a ready "handle."

If you have a good grip on your opponent's hair, you control the movement of his head. If you control the movement of his head, you control his balance. The leverage achieved is tremendous. Wherever his hair goes, he goes. It may sound like a comic image, and it can be that, on stage, but it is also true. With that good grip you can force your opponent to the floor or force him to move in any direction from a standing position. And although you often cannot lift people off the floor by their hair, because they weigh too much, you can make it so painful for them by pulling upward that you create "an irresistible urge" for them to get themselves up.

Okay, you say, if I keep talking about men and battlefield conditions, why is this a special technique for women? Well, as I noted above, it really isn't. It is asexual in usage and technique. However, most of the plays performed in the United States each year are modern scripts. By that I mean Ibsen and later. The periods in which they are set are ones in which fashion dictates that the male characters have short hair and the women have long or longish hair. This means that battles between men will usually not involve hair as a factor. The same mores dictate that women can use hair as a weapon when battling. Therefore, most of the time, if hair-pulling is a factor, it is a woman assailant going after a woman victim. Incidentally, in terms of 1970s' hairstyles for both men and women, the leverage achieved when a person grabs a good handful of hair on a victim makes this a very credible and advantageous move to use when you want a woman to subdue a male in stage business.

How do you do it? Very simply. You reach out and grab a handful of hair. BUT DON'T PULL! As I explained above, the leverage involved when you control a person's hair is very great. If you really pull the victim's hair you will a) ruin the character's hairstyle for ensuing scenes; b) leave her with a very sore scalp; and c) most important of all, throw her off-balance. So, don't do it. Use isometrics to create the illusion of pulling the victim's hair, but in reality "zero it out." For men, and for "mixed doubles," the same ground rules apply.

Scratching

First of all, stay away from the eyes. You have no margin for error and a sharp fingernail will act on the eyeball like a knife. Even if you chew your nails down to the quick, your blunt fingertip will do damage.

That understood, the technique is simple:

1) Curl the hand and fingers so that the

flat surface of the second knuckle of each finger, not the fingernails, "rakes" across the victim's face.

2) Make sure the motion is parallel to the victim's face, not angled into it to any large degree. This way you can draw your knuckles across the face (or other designated surface) quite rapidly without actually striking the victim. Realize that the curled hand is a semi-balled fist. If you slap that *into* the victim's face you will hurt him.

3) Make sure the motion is fairly rapid. If you: a) "claw" your hand; b) get it up to the victim's face and make initial gentle contact of knuckle surface to skin surface; and c) draw the knuckles rapidly down or across the victim's face and follow through the action, which will take the hand away from the face, then the audience will never catch you faking it, no matter how close to you they are.

4) The victim, of course, must react phys-ically and vocally in a manner that sustains the illusion.

Choking

Choking is truly an asexual, bisexual, cross-sexual piece of stage violence. It is included in this section for convenience. Choking often comes in the middle of, or as the climax to, a fight scene that has been in progress. Usually, one character has to subdue and/or stabilize the other before the action can commence. It is hard to choke a moving target. There are obvious exceptions: a great disparity in size and strength between the assailant and the victim, surprise attack, a sleeping victim, or a victim who will not or cannot defend herself. In those cases, the violence can commence with the act of choking.

The main thing to remember is to stay away from the windpipe! Incidents are legion where "staged" choking left an actor or actress blue in the face and unconscious. It takes very little pressure to close off the air passage.

1) Wrap your hands around the victim's neck with your fingers at the rear of the neck and your thumbs aligned on the victim's collarbone. As long as those thumbs are on the collarbone the illusion is sustained, and so is the victim's breath.

2) Do not put any pressure on the collarbone with your thumbs. *Pull* with the fingers at the back of the victim's neck.

3) Press downward with your wrists so that the heel of your palm goes against the victim's chest (2 and 3 should pretty much cancel each other out).

4) Use your shoulders, arms, etc., in isometric opposition on the victim.

5) The victim provides physical and emotional reaction on her own to sustain the illusion.

Figure 30 *Scratching*

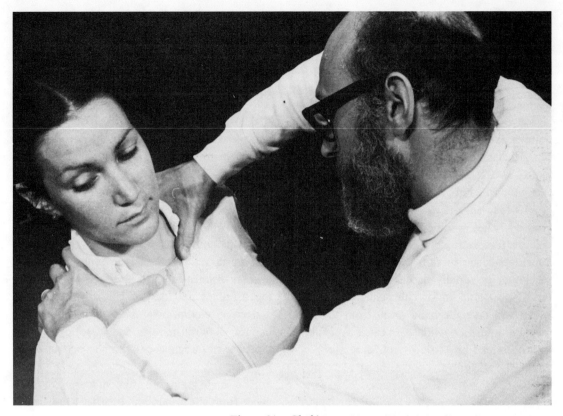

Figure 31 *Choking*

Summary

The whole question of formal "gentlemen's rules" of combat versus "battlefield" or "street" conditions will be gone into in Chapter VI. Suffice it to say that except in certain scenes where a formal boxing or wrestling match is called for, all unarmed combat is informal. The nature of the characters and the dramatic situation will determine whether the characters fight "clean" or "dirty." Depending on your aesthetic decision, the audience will see clumsy (or graceful) grappling between two angered but untrained men, or trained combatants employing one or more of the martial arts. That, as noted earlier, is a matter of style.

In using any of the techniques outlined in this chapter, however, certain rules remain in force:

1) The assailant provides motivation only. The victim always provides his own impetus. Both must always maintain their own balance and have control of their own bodies.

2) Both assailant and victim must use isometrics to create the illusion of struggle. The pressure brought to bear by each on each should be as closely "zeroed out" as possible to assure the maintainance of balance.

3) All initial planning and rehearsing must be done on a gym mat.

4) When dealing with the judo-wrestling throws, the final stages must be done at full speed from the start. From the moment the victim leaves his feet to roll down the ramp, slow motion is impossible. Up to that point, and with all other sections of this chapter, start rehearsal in slow motion, making sure you have set your space relationships, foot placement, angle of attack, and all other factors in place. Slowly increase the speed with

which the move is practiced, making sure you are kinesthetically secure with each step of the move, and at each level of speed, before going on to the next.

5) Practice the entire move, at full speed, both on the mat and then on the hard stage floor, out of the context of the scene, until you are kinesthetically secure. Only then will you be ready to "act" it in the context of character and dramatic action.

Chapter VI

KNIFE HANDLING

THEORY AND PRACTICE FOR THE STAGE

Knife handling is one of the most chilling and frightening types of action you can work with on the stage. This is true for both the audience and for the performers who are doing the business. There seems to be an atavistic fear in most of us about knives, about blades in general. One can kill impersonally with a gun. There is some distance between the assailant and the victim when the weapon is a spear, a bayonet, or even a sword. But a knife—that's different. A knife can only be used close to the victim. You have to touch him, feel his body receive and react to the wound. If the puncture turns into a rip or gash, he's going to bleed all over you. A knife is very personal, and because we feel this instinctively, knife work is very tricky on the stage. If it is done well the audience will gasp in empathetic horror. If it is done badly and the illusion is broken, the audience will most likely laugh. The tension created in an audience by the appearance of that blade is so strong that it must be released and resolved, either through empathetic horror or through the relief of laughter. Dramatically, there is no margin for error.

Depending on the script, you may be holding a hunting knife, a carving knife, a penknife, a letter opener, an ice pick, an icicle, a hatpin, a spindle, a shard of glass, or whatever other long, sharp instrument the mind of man can conceive and invent. For our purposes it does not matter. In all of these cases it looks like a knife. It is being handled like a knife. It will have the same effect as a knife.

In terms of safety, the margin for error, while present, is never enormous. Knives must be handled with great care. What should you use? I would recommend a real steel blade, blunt but real. A rubber-bladed prop knife creates no illusion whatever. You are better off leaving it in its "sheath" and strangling the victim with your bare hands. Property knives with blades of plastic or wood are visually effective if well built. However, they are just as stiff and sharp as the blunt steel blade and they will penetrate the body just as easily if there is an error in judgment, if they meet the body at precisely the "right" angle, or if an actor falls upon them. Further, precisely because they are plastic or wood and not "real," there is often a tendency to handle them carelessly, to play with them. "After all," says the actor, moments before the accident, "it's only a prop." Prop it may be, but it will kill or maim just as quickly as steel. When the actor has steel in his hand, he is a little nervous about it. He knows how dangerous it is and is not likely to delude himself that it is "only a prop". Steel presents no more danger than plastic or wood. It looks better. And it does wonders for an actor's concentration!

What about the property knives you can buy with a spring-loaded handle? Press the blade against anything and the blade retreats into the handle. That's the theory. What happens if the spring sticks? I've seen it happen. The assailant slams the blade home into the victim's chest or back, secure in the knowledge that the blade is going up into the handle, not down into flesh. It's not his fault that the spring would not move, or that it got hung up half-way back. The likelihood of the spring's failing, if it has been tested just before being brought on stage, is not very great. Nevertheless, it is always a possibility. For that reason, I suggest you stay away from spring-loaded knives.

Use a real knife. Be sure it is blunt to reduce the chance of accidental nicks and cuts from people simply touching the blade. Be sure it is clean and rust-free. If skin is broken, you don't want to increase the chance of tetanus. Handle with care.

How to Hold and Handle the Weapon

On preparing for stage action

How do you hold and handle a knife? As little as possible! The knife should never be touched by anyone except the master of properties and the actor who is to use it on stage. No one else should ever pick it up, for *any* reason. Anyone else found handling the weapon should be severely reprimanded, and if he does it a second time he should be removed from the cast. The actor who is to handle the weapon removes it from the properties table only to bring it on stage, and returns it to the properties table immediately upon exiting from the stage. If the actor has a quick change, then the properties master or his designee should be waiting at the exit to receive the knife from the actor and return it to the properties table.

The knife should be sheathed or encased whenever possible. This means always when it is on the properties table, and whenever character costume and situation permit the actor to keep it sheathed. Sometimes this is impossible. The scissors used for the death weapon in *Dial M for Murder* need to be preset "naked" on the desk, but they should rest in a case on the properties table at all other times. If a character who carries a knife *can* carry it in a sheath, please have him do so. If a switchblade knife or jackknife can be carried closed, please do so. Until the moment comes for the blade to be used, it should be shielded to prevent an accident.

When you are carrying an unshielded blade to the stage, and whenever possible (consistent with character) while carrying it on stage, carry the blade point down. Always know where the point of that blade is, and be sure that it is away from your own body. If the point is toward your body and you trip over a light cable or a piece of furniture and fall, you may be severely injured.

If the point is away from your body and you walk into someone or they fall against you, or if someone simply walks up behind you or backs into you, they can wind up with several inches of the blade planted somewhere in their anatomy. But if that blade is pointed down toward the floor, then any of the above things can happen and the worst consequence possible is that the knife blade will bury itself in, and possibly snap off in, the floor. The worst consequence is that you will need a new prop.

In action on stage

The ease and dexterity with which you handle the blade will depend on your character. The inexperienced or panicky weapon holder will grasp the handle tightly with the pommel extending past his thumb and the blade emerging from the bottom of his gripping hand. He will attempt to strike overhand. This seems to be the "classic" stabbing action —which it is—but it is awkward and clumsy. It leaves the knife-wielder open to quick and effective counteraction by the would-be victim. Such a blow can be easily blocked, and the knife-wielder's own body is wide open should the victim have a weapon of his own or wish to employ a knee, fist, or foot. This grip on the knife, and the accompanying overhand arc of

Figure 32 *How to hold a knife*

the blow, will work fine if the victim is: a) un-conscious and/or immobile; b) physically restrained or emotionally frozen in position; or c) serenely unaware of the assailant's presence and/or intention.

In such cases, the experienced and/or sadistic knife-wielder can use the above grip and arc to great effect. If the victim is ready and able to fight back, such a grip and arc are ineffectual.

The proper way to hold a knife for a fight is to let the handle rest balanced across your up-turned palm and fingers; the heel of the handle resting on the heel of your hand, above the pinky, and the rest of the handle lying diagonally across the jointure of your ring finger and the hand, the third knuckle of your middle finger and the second knuckle of your index finger. Your thumb pins the handle against your palm and fingers. Your wrist is loose and flexible. The point is toward your opponent. Try it. See how flexibly and easily you can move the point of the blade with your fingers and your wrist. Do not curl your fingers tightly over the handle until you are ready to "stab." Then you do close your grip firmly, to provide rigidity. With your grip tight and your wrist locked, you restrict considerably both the scope and quickness of the blade's action. With the light grip described above:

a) It is very easy to keep your knife point between your body and your opponent's blade. It is a good defensive position.

b) You have maximum flexibility to dart through any opening in your opponent's guard to "stab" any target area on his body.

c) Whether your opponent is armed or not, the darting, weaving, dancing point of your knife-blade made possible with this grip and minimal wrist action is an incredibly effective piece of dramatic business—almost hypnotic in its effect.

All slashes, feints, stabs, etc., deriving from this grip are underhand or sidearm. Remember, a tight grasp on the handle with this underhand grip will look awkward and clumsy, and you will find it difficult to manipulate the blade in a graceful and menacing manner. Relax your hand and wrist and let the blade move.

Obviously if you are handling a heavy, unbalanced bread knife or a pair of sewing shears, you can't balance it on your palm and fingers. Take a good firm underhand grip, as described above, and start from there.

I have seen a third grip which is very effective, but which I do not recommend for stage combat. It was taught to a Special Forces friend of mine by South Korean troops in Indochina, and he taught it to me. The knife handle is held in a tight grip with the pommel of the handle circled by thumb and forefinger and the blade extending from the bottom of the hand. However, the knife is held shoulder-high with the heel of the knife hand facing the opponent and the sharpened edge of the blade, instead of the point, facing the opponent. Your blade is parallel to your body. Only slashing movements are used, never stabbing motions, and the motion is made by snapping and recocking the wrist. The arc of the blade is very quick and short and is almost always aimed at the opponent's face and neck area, although you can slash at an attacking arm or hand as well. There are two problems with this grip for stage purposes. First, the primary motion is slashing and we need to be able to stab. Second, and more important, the blade is carried high and its primary target areas are the face and neck. This is terribly unsafe. It is also impossible to mask this motion from the audience. Therefore, you cannot allow a proper margin of safety, through masking, in performing the action on stage. For these reasons, I recommend against using this knife technique in a stage-combat situation. It can be very effective in a solo demonstration of technique by a character, as long as he is not within arm's reach of anyone else.

Notes: 1) Regardless of the grip employed, always be sure that the attacking motions (feint, slash, stab, etc.) are targeted for your opponent's shoulder or below. Never, ever, even feint at the face or throat. The consequences of error are too great. All cutting or stabbing motions *must* be targeted lower than the collarbone.

2) When circling, feinting, and otherwise working your way through the choreography toward the moment of the thrust that will end the fight, stay at least one arm's length away from your opponent. This is the same principle stated in Chapter IV that you do not plan a righthand blow to the jaw to go through the space vacated by the victim's reaction. You plan it to go by and miss clean, if close. In the same way, you may wish to plan a "slash" from which the opponent darts back and clear. If the blade is planned to go through vacated space you are risking an injury. Make sure the blade's arc is one that misses the opponent even if he is late in darting backward.

3) All preliminary motions, moves, and blows with the knife should be slashing rather than stabbing motions. The first strong stabbing motion we should see, toward the opponent's body, should be the last motion of the encounter. A knife thrust straight toward your partner's body is the ultimate in risk on stage. In the next section I will show you how to convert the thrust to a perfectly safe move, a move that requires masking. If you have not closed with your opponent, you cannot mask the procedure with your body. That would leave you with a choice either of thrusting your point at your partner's body—a move that admits zero margin for error and has potentially lethal consequences—or of "faking it" *with* an adequate margin, in which case you have no illusion of danger. You can't thrust

close enough to look real without taking a tremendous risk. Leave it out!

CREATING THE ILLUSION OF STABBING AND WITHDRAWAL OF THE WEAPON

When attempting to stab someone in real life, you approach the victim with the blade perpendicular to his body and attempt to penetrate. When staging the illusion of a stabbing:

Step 1) Mask the stabbing with your own body or with the victim's. Do not stand in absolute profile where the audience can clearly see the hand action. In arena, complete the masking by bringing your body against the victim with the knife between you.

Step 2) As you complete the masking, pivot the blade in your hand so that it is *parallel* to the victim's body, not perpendicular.

Step 3) Punch the victim's body with your knuckles, which are around the hilt of the knife. This gives the illusion of the knife's being driven home.

Step 4) According to the nature of the character and the situation, you may wish to do more than puncture the victim's body. With your knuckles pressed into the victim and the blade pivoted parallel between you, use isometric tension for the effort of ripping the blade up, down, or sideways while it is still within the body. This is a vicious movement. It can further delineate character. It also "guarantees death," whereas a simple puncture wound may not.

Step 5) When you withdraw the blade:

    a) Employ isometrics to make the "withdrawal" require effort. Blades do not come out as easily as they go in.

    b) Snap your wrist back to present to the audience the momentary view of the blade perpendicular to the victim's body again.

    c) Then mask the blade from the audience until it has been

       cleaned, sheathed, or disposed of, so that they cannot see the absence of blood on the blade.

    d) The victim must fall so as to mask the absence of blood where he has been stabbed.

Suppose you *want* blood on the blade. This is a problem for costume and makeup. Let the designer prepare a "blood-packet." Do not attempt to cut it open with the blade of the knife; you risk cutting the costume and the actor in the process. The blood-packet can be designed to rupture from the pressure of your knuckles around the handle of the knife as you are "ripping" (Step 4). It can be slit open with a burr on the ring you are wearing for that purpose on the knife hand. Once the packet is ruptured, and the blood has poured out, then bring the knife blade across its flow before Step 5. You'll have a bloody blade to display if that's what you want, and the victim can fall any way he wants, to display the wound for the audience.

A little blood can be effective in a realistic production. In a stylized production, such as a *Hamlet* set in its own time, I would not bother even with that. A great deal of blood, no matter how convincingly you can motivate it in your own mind, is likely to create a gory mess that will drive the audience right out of their emotional participation in the play. Beware of overdoing this. If they believe it's the actor's blood, you will scare them out of the theatre. If it's obvious that it is makeup, and they do not believe, then they are likely to laugh *you* right out of the theatre.

Suppose you don't want to withdraw the blade, but want to leave it sticking in the "corpse." First of all, you can't use Steps 1 to 5. You need a different technique. You have a costume problem rather than a stage violence illusion. The victim's chest or back is thoroughly protected with sizable metal breastplates or backplates worn under the costume. Then the portion of the anatomy in question is

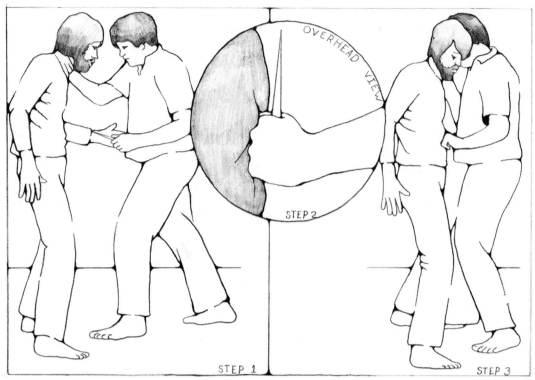

Figure 33　*The illusion of stabbing, Steps 1, 2, and 3*

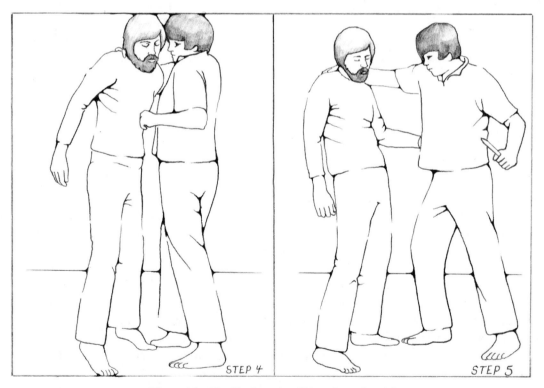

Figure 34　*The illusion of stabbing, Steps 4 and 5*

built up with dermawax, or a similar substance, so that a false, secondary chest or back and shoulder is created. You can bury a blood-packet in the proper spot if you wish. The area must be built up carefully so that it looks real; then it is covered with clothes (or makeup, if he is to be bare-chested), and you are ready. The stab wound goes straight into the victim and penetrates in the center of the area protected by the metal plate. The knife should be angled in so that several inches of the blade can be buried in a couple of inches of dermawax. Then just let go of the blade. It will stick.

PHYSIOLOGICAL ACTION AND REACTION TO BEING STABBED

The person being stabbed, the victim, has to do his part, as well. Unless the victim is secure and comfortable with the business, the audience will find itself watching an actor trying not to be stabbed rather than a character who is being stabbed or slashed. The technique needs to be rehearsed many, many times in slow motion until everyone is comfortable. The physiological and emotional action and reaction to that knife should be the character's, not the performer's.

Once the performers are comfortable with the business and have confidence in it, and in each other, what we have is an acting problem. How you will react to being stabbed will depend on: a) where you have been stabbed; b) what weapon was used and how sharp it was; c) the dimensions of the wound; and d) your emotional awareness of the knife and your own physical state.

The various areas of the body have a widely differentiated number of nerve endings per square inch of skin. Sensitive areas such as the fingertips or the palm are packed with sensory nerve endings. Therefore, a cut in those areas would be quite painful. The abdomen has relatively few nerve endings; so does the back. In terms of a simple puncture wound, a sharp blade could be in and out and you

wouldn't know it or recognize it for what it was until you started to feel the internal pain resulting from the damage of the blade, until the air hit the wound, and/or until you became aware of the flow of blood. This means a delay of anywhere from half a second if the blade reached a vital organ to several minutes if there was no essential damage done and your own adrenalin was pumping like mad. If the blade pierced the heart, you might still have not felt it enter the body, as there are few nerve endings in the center of the chest. But when it sliced into the heart, it caused heart failure and that is what you are reacting to. As the heart beats a little more than once a second, it would be a second or two before the heart failure convulsed the body. So the first questions to ask in determining your response are where did the blade go in? How far? What damage has been done? Have any of my functions been impaired? (For example in Act V, Scene i of Shakespeare's *Othello,* Cassio is stabbed in the leg by Iago. How badly? Can he still walk? Will the leg bear weight? Can he run? Can he fight?)

Second, you need to know what weapon was used and how sharp it was. A dull knife or a piece of jagged glass don't slice through flesh; they rip. Because the progress of such a weapon is relatively slow and erratic, because it must be forced into the body and through its passage, the weapon will have to be wielded with a great deal of isometric "strength" and it will cause a great deal of pain as it goes through. A sharp blade, with a sharp point, goes in very quickly and easily. A victim can actually be unaware of its presence until the result of its entry makes itself felt. Basically, what the victim would feel first would be the impact of the assailant's hand and/or hilt as the blade is driven home. It would feel like a slap on the back (or abdomen). The second thing he would feel, in a rapid "in and out" puncture wound, would be an unfamiliar breeze as the outside air hit the new wound and the nerve endings along the passage of the blade. Then the victim would start to feel pain commensurate with the location, severity, and dimension of the wound.

Third, you have to decide the nature and dimension of the wound. In the case of a rip, once the blade had penetrated the body, there is no question that you could feel it and that it would disable you completely. On the other end of the scale, a simple puncture wound could come and go, if you were in the heat of battle, and you would not know it until the effect of the wound made itself known. The same is true for a simple flesh wound on the arm or leg, breast, back, or shoulder. As long as these cuts and slashes did not sever muscle or tendons and disable the part in question, you could legitimately ignore them. How should you react to the wound? How severe is it? When do you become aware of it? How big is it, how noticeable, under the circumstances? Let me give you a concrete example. The Earl of Warwick in Shakespeare's *Henry VI, Part III* enters in Act V, Scene ii, severely wounded on the field of battle, and dies after a twenty-five-line speech. We know he is wounded, but where, how? What is he dying of? If he has a battle-ax sticking out of his liver, he will have a hard time saying one line, let alone twenty-five, before passing on to his reward. Suppose you can't spare two extras in your production to carry him on, and you want him to enter under his own power? Warwick has been in hand-to-hand combat all day. You can work on the premise that he has won each of his encounters but has been wounded in many of them. You can play him disabled if you have a litter to carry him in on, and extras to carry it. If not, then assume that he does not have any severe leg wounds, because that way he can stagger in on his own feet. He has a *series* of wounds, all of them minor, but all of them bleeding, and he is dying from loss of blood. In the kaleidoscope of battle that precedes Warwick's death speech, you can have him wounded several times and he can ignore or override each of the wounds. You plan the severity and dimensions of the wound according to the needs of the character at that moment in the script, and then react accordingly.

Finally, your reaction will be affected by your awareness of the blade, and by your physiological condition. As I said at the opening of the chapter, almost all of us have an atavistic fear of blades. There is no good way to be hurt and no good way to die; but being torn up with a blade is one of the most terrifying ways we can think of. If your character sees the blade coming and knows he is about to be stabbed, he is most likely to be very frightened and terribly aware of being stabbed even before the blade enters his flesh. The anticipation of injury, of pain, and of death will magnify the first two in the mind and feelings of the victim. Nothing can magnify the last. Just as you can feel the dentist's drill before you even get in the chair, so, too, can you feel the blade entering your body before it even makes contact. Delayed reactions to stab wounds are predicated on surprise, on the victim's not knowing it was coming. Where there is foreknowledge, there is usually anticipation of pain, of feeling, of terror on the part of the victim. There are some exceptions such as Brutus at the moment of his suicide in Shakespeare's *Julius Caesar*. To him death is welcome and the sword is a friend. But such cases are rare, and I think the few exceptions support the rule of thumb.

Your emotional and physiological condition is a factor, particularly if you are in the heat of battle. When the body is geared up for combat it can withstand shocks that it could not accept under normal circumstances. Thus, Warwick, above, can sustain many small wounds and ignore them. Had he cut himself with a scythe on his estate in Warwickshire he would have attended to the wound immediately, and he would have sworn a great deal at the discomfort it caused him, too. This is how a Marine can continue to take part in a fire-fight with twenty pieces of shrapnel in him. As long as the wounds haven't broken a bone, severed a tendon, or interfered with heart-lung functions, etc., the Marine continues to fire; Warwick continues to wield his sword. Only after the battle is over does the body wind down enough that normal pain and other nerve reactions take over again.

It seems, then, that your reaction to a knife attack will depend on the nature of the weapon; the location, nature, and severity of the wound; your character's awareness of the blade before it entered his body, and your character's mental and emotional state at the moment the blade entered. Emotional reaction is a matter of interpretation between actor and director. For physiological reaction, when in doubt, ask your doctor. He can give you a sound medical basis on which to plan the physical business.

SUMMARY

There is no more dangerous a sequence of business in the realm of stage violence than that of the knife attack. There are few that are *as* dangerous. Your margin of safety depends on the maturity, solemnity, and care with which this piece of stage business is handled by your cast. No procedure devised by man will protect an actor from carelessness, stupidity, or adolescent "horsing around," on his own part or on the part of another:

1) Knives and their counterparts (razors, ice picks, scissors, etc.) are to be handled only for the purpose of rehearsal and performance —never "for fun."

2) Plan your spacing of bodies and feet, the angle of attack, the masking of the blow, and the timing of everything with exquisite care. Take all the time you need to plan this down to the millisecond and millimeter. Never, ever tell your performers to "go work it out." You, the director or fight coach, work it out with them. It must be choreographed.

3) Be aware of the space around the action. Keep other actors clear of the knife as the assailant moves it around.

4) Make sure there is little or no oppor-

tunity for the actors engaged in a knife fight or knife attack to stumble on furniture, cords, capes, or the train or hem of a dress. Make sure the assailant and victim always know where they are in relation to all set pieces and set furniture, so that they do not stumble on platforms, ramps, steps, etc.

5) Make sure a blade is accounted for before someone holding one falls to the ground. Close it. Sheathe it. Put it down. Drop it upstage, away from the audience, and clear of the area where the fall will take place. You don't want to risk a fall with a naked blade in the actor's possession. Get rid of it before he goes down. If you must fall with, or fall on, a knife in the course of a play, then do a left side-fall, rolling over onto your stomach. As you start the fall, hold the blade firmly in your right fist, with your wrist turned so that the blade is parallel to your body, and the flat side of the blade is pressed against you. As you start to roll from your side onto your stomach, slide your right hand sufficiently across your torso so that the pointed tip of the knife is clear of your rib cage on the left side. The knife point may touch the stage floor as you roll over but it will be clear of your torso. I don't like this move, and I don't recommend it. You ought to find some other solution for the "accidental self-stabbing." If you are stubborn enough to insist on this move, however, the above will likely get you through.

6) Practice in slow motion, at half speed, again and again until everyone involved in knife handling is completely kinesthetically secure. Then speed it up gradually until you are doing it, out of context, at full speed, with full kinesthetic security.

7) Never plan or allow any blade movement in the area of the face and throat. All movement must be shoulders and below from the back and side; collarbone and below from the front.

Always, at all times, handle knives with care and respect.

Chapter VII

THE USE OF WEAPONS

"Weapon" is a broad descriptive term. It can refer to a hand-held antiaircraft missile wielded by a combat infantryman, or to a hefty rock in the possession of a Cro-Magnon. It can refer to a wide variety of objects and missiles in between these two extremes. In this chapter we shall deal with three ideas: a) the theory of weapons use on stage in terms of safety; b) the proper selection of weapons in terms both of character and of dramatic effectiveness; and c) how to find the proper choreographic approach to the use and clash of weapons that will reflect character and situation. There is, for example, a tremendous difference in style between court fencing for pleasure in Shakespeare's Elsinore castle (*Hamlet,* Act V), in amateur competition in contemporary colleges and universities, and in the handling of those same weapons on a battlefield or "in the street." We shall explore that difference.

Theory and Practice for the Stage

The first and most important thing to be said about weapons is that they are tools of the performer; they are not toys! They must be handled carefully and with respect. In dealing with any weapon that has a cutting or stabbing edge, no matter how dull or how blunted, you are dealing with a potentially lethal weapon. All of the precautions enumerated in Chapter VI for the safe handling of knives should be in force here. Only the person using the weapon should handle it and only when he is going on stage. This applies to thrusting weapons, cutting weapons, bludgeoning weapons—all weapons!

Any sharp blade should be sheathed or encased whenever possible. When carrying the weapon to or from the stage, and when carrying it on the stage, be aware of the extra reach a sword or spear has over a knife. If you tuck it under your arm it can pierce a person a couple of feet away from you. Carry it point down!

Never "improvise" with a weapon. Every moment of weapon use on stage must be completely planned, meticulously rehearsed, and kinesthetically learned before it is inserted into a rehearsal of the scene.

It does not matter how much armor an actor is wearing. A weapon is always dangerous. Isometrics is an integral part of weapons handling for the stage. Even though the blow is supposed to be blocked by your opponent's weapon or shield, there is always the possibility that he will forget or be confused and make the wrong defensive move, or be *late* with the right defensive move. If these errors occur, your stage partner stands to be badly hurt. If a weapon blow is choreographed to miss your partner, or if its arc will take the weapon past him if he fails to make the right counterblow with his own weapon or shield, then you may swing away to your heart's content. Otherwise, use isometrics and control that blow. Be prepared to stop it dead in its tracks, or as close to that as humanly possible with a heavy weapon such as a two-hand broadsword, if your partner fails to make the right response.

Okay, once you are on the stage and ready to rehearse, where do we go from there? As in Chapters III and IV, the simplest approach is to discuss separately weapons aimed at the body and weapons aimed at the head.

Body blows

Weapons fall into three categories:

a) Ballistic weapons, such as firearms, slingshots, bow and arrow, etc. With the exception of the arrow, none of the missiles is visible in flight, or as it leaves the discharging weapon, or as it strikes the victim. You can see an arrow being drawn on the bow. You can see it sticking out of the victim. Using an arrow on stage is a special-effects problem, not one of combat safety. You no more shoot a real arrow at a victim than you would fire a real bullet. In handling a slingshot the solution is obvious: pantomime. The assailant never really "loads" the slingshot with a rock. Obviously in all ballistic weapons cases, no real missile is employed, so we are dealing with pantomime on the part of both assailant and victim. Therefore safety factors, though present, are minimal and are related more to the preparation of the weapon than to its handling by the actor to simulate the firing of the weapon. Firearms are a different matter, and definite safety procedures are involved. See Chapter X for details.

b) Stabbing weapons such as knives, swords, spears, bayonets, etc. The solutions for knives have already been discussed. The technique of the snapped wrist and the masking described in Chapter VI for knife handling are not possible with the longer weapons. They cannot be hidden, or masked, between the bodies of the actors. They have to simulate going into or through the victim's body. The old tried and true solution of passing between the victim's arm and side at about elbow height is still the best one. There are a few additions that will help create the illusion for you:

1) Thrust the weapon under the victim's upstage arm. In terms of the audience's line of sight, it will appear to have gone through the body.

2) Don't leave the blade "in" the victim very long. Thrust it in, allow the victim to react (one or two beats), and then withdraw the weapon. It will be "in and out" before the audience decides to find out where the weapon truly is. Of course they know the weapon has not gone through the victim; however, they have given themselves over to the play (we hope) and are willing to accept the illusion you have created, as long as you do not make them look at an actor staggering about in his death-agony with a broadsword tucked under his armpit. Get the weapon out fast!

If you are in arena and there is no upstage, the technique will still work if the thrust and withdrawal are one sequential motion with no delay. If the weapon goes "in-out"—that fast —the audience will *feel* it, empathetically, much more than they will *see* it.

One good solution, in arena, is to get your victim on the floor before thrusting the weapon "through" his body. You can thus place the assailant's body between the audience seated to the assailant's back and the weapon. You then thrust the weapon into the floor next to the victim's body, and either the victim or the assailant is between the audience and the weapon. There is some masking for everyone. This helps, but not as much as one would like, so you still want a pretty rapid "in and out" to prevent the illusion from dissolving.

3) Remember that a weapon that has been thrust into the victim's body is entangled in muscle, bone, and tendon. It doesn't come out nearly as easily as it went in. You will want to employ a greater degree of isometric tension and effort to pull the blade free than you employed to thrust it in. If you are dealing with a one-hand weapon, you may want to use the other hand to push the victim away, off the blade, as you pull it out. If you are dealing with a long sword or a two-hand weapon, you

may want to place a foot against the victim (sole flat to the body) and thrust him backward while "pulling" the weapon free with your hands. This is an easier move when the victim is on the floor, but it can be employed when he is upright and provide the impetus for him to take his fall. Please remember when utilizing this that you are to provide motivation only. You do not really thrust with your foot. You isometrically pretend to.

c) The third category is impact weapons such as clubs, maces, pool cues, baseball bats, lead pipe, or pieces of lumber, stone, or metal. Delivering a blow to the body with one of these weapons is exactly the same as delivering it with the hand holding the weapon. If the wrist and elbow are locked, the weapon is merely an extension of the hand, and the seven steps for body blows outlined in Chapter III apply. Substitute the word "weapon" for "fist" as you go through the steps, and be sure the weapon reaches the victim's skin with zero foot-pounds of impact. The reaction to the attack will vary with the weapon. How heavy is it? How hard were you hit? Where did it land? If it is a hard and blunt instrument, the reaction is similar to being punched or kicked, only you have been hit harder.

The idea of "in and out" applies here too; but, because the body can double over the weapon, you have an option. You can isometrically land on the front or back of the victim's body, allow one or two beats for reaction, and then snap the weapon back from the victim. If you have hit him in the back you need to do this. If the blow landed in his stomach, you can follow the same procedure. You can alternatively have the victim double over the weapon or wrap his arms around it, thus holding it in place as the actors complete their reaction to the blow.

Head blows

The same three categories of ballistic weapons, stabbing weapons, and impact weapons apply here as in the preceding section on Body blows. Because ballistic weapons are simulated in their contact with the victim, no special dangers are involved where the head region is concerned, and all notes in the Ballistic section above apply here, too. The problems of safety related to head blows with either a stabbing or an impact weapon are the same. It is safe to plan head blows, pursuant to the above suggestions, with any part of the assailant's body. It is safe to plan head blows with weapons that are blocked by the victim's own weapon as part of the fight choreography. Planning blows to the head with a weapon, which are intended to land or to simulate landing, is in my opinion a very risky business and to be avoided if at all possible.

If you are dealing with a prop candlestick or chair leg that is actually a balsa wood "breakaway," you are relatively safe. But remember that a "breakaway" weapon just might not do so, and use isometric control.

To strike the head with a real length of pipe or a blackjack is flirting with disaster no matter how well the blow is rehearsed. A miscalculation in those circumstances can have fatal consequences.

THE CHOOSING OF WEAPONS

There are two kinds of considerations you must be aware of in selecting weapons for your production, always providing the playwright has given you a choice: 1) the historical period; and 2) the nature, social class, and purpose of the character who is armed.

The historical period

If you were doing a realistic production that involved American Civil War soldiers, and you brought them on stage in proper 1860 uniform carrying M-16 rifles from the 1960's, you would have a ludicrous situation, and you would be instantly aware of it. So would your audience. It is too close for them, in time-frame, and the anachronism is immediately recognizable. On the other hand, if you were to do a relatively antiquarian production of *Coriolanus,* set in Roman times, and you used a Greek short sword instead of a Roman gladius (the Roman infantry's short sword), it is highly unlikely that the audience would notice.

You are dealing with a value judgment and an aesthetic judgment on the part of the producer and the director. How sophisticated is your audience? What standard of historical accuracy are you used to? What standard is your audience used to? What resources do you have to acquire weapons by rental or building? What weapons are available to you, given your resources? If we are dealing with the Guthrie Theatre in Minneapolis, or the Festival Theatre in Stratford (Canada *or* England), the costumer, armorer, actor, and director would all rather die than bring a Greek sword on in the hands of a Roman general. The level of expectation is much too high for that, and properly so. If you are dealing with a civic theatre in Tecumseh, Michigan; a high school in Omaha, Nebraska; or a college with a respectable but nonprofessional theatre, it is another matter. Perhaps neither the company nor the audience will be too fussy, and, I would say, properly so. Of course we want exactly the right weapon, if we can get it. If not, we have to make do, within limits. The goal is historical accuracy. Your flexibility in meeting this goal is limited only by what is credible to your company and your audience.

Sometimes the playwright throws you a curve in terms of historical accuracy. In *Hamlet,* Shakespeare required, or at least intended, that Hamlet and Laertes duel with rapier and dagger (Act V, Scene ii, lines 151–152). But these are 16th-century weapons, the weapons of Shakespeare's time. The play is set at least four hundred years earlier, in a time when rapier and dagger were unknown. The proper weapon for the period was a heavy sword with a blade about 36 inches long and 1 inch wide,

and a circular buckler. Why didn't Shakespeare's audience object? Because he was consistent. All of Shakespeare's plays were performed in the costume of his own time, with only small indicative costume pieces to indicate the stated era and location. *Hamlet,* set in 11th-century Denmark; *A Midsummer Night's Dream,* set in ancient Athens; and *Julius Caesar, Coriolanus,* and *Antony and Cleopatra,* all set in Roman times, were played in Elizabethan costume. That being the case, Elizabethan weapons for *Hamlet* are not anachronistic. If you play *Hamlet* in 20th-century garb, you have the choice of using guns, collegiate fencing foils, rapier and dagger, or switchblade knives. All are credible, if not desirable. If you play it in Elizabethan costume, rapier and dagger is possible and will work. If you use Middle Ages setting and costume, however, you ought to use a reasonable counterpart in the choice of weapons.

Incidentally, audiences are much more sophisticated now than ever before. Higher levels of education and films and television have made the average person much more aware of other times and places. Your audience may not be able to say why the weapons look wrong ("My goodness, Harry, he's carrying a hoplite spear [Greek infantry] and he's supposed to be a Roman soldier!"). However, they have probably seen so many costume epics that they do realize that somehow it looks wrong, especially if your weapons are too far out of keeping with the setting of the play.

How far is "too far"? I can't tell you. I can only repeat: try for complete accuracy, and, failing that, get as close as you can, given your resources. If I cannot have exactly what I ought to have, and I must choose between a beautifully balanced weapon from an associated period, with a good ring of steel, on the one hand, and a perfect historical replica with a bad, tinny blade on the other, I will choose to violate period in order to be able to choreograph a rousing good fight where the blades look and sound authentic as they come together. If an 18th-century pirate's cutlass is all I can get for a medieval knight, I think I would rather do without any sword and find him another weapon. I'd make him a period spear from a broom handle and a painted wood blade and stage a quarter-staff fight!

There is a tremendous diversity of weapons to choose from, warfare being one of man's most imaginative occupations. I recommend you to the art books in the local library for pictures, plates, and portraits of the warriors of all ages preserved in statuary, frescoes, and paintings. The Metropolitan Museum of Art in New York City has a splendid armor and weapons collection, as do many other museums. If you are to choose your weapons wisely, do some research. It won't take you long to find examples of the one or two pieces you are looking for.

The nature, social class, and purpose of the character

A weapon is an extension of a man. The kind of person he is, the way he reacts to other people, his standing in society and his own perception of that standing, and his satisfaction (or lack of it) with his standing, all are reflected in the way he arms himself and the way he handles that weapon.

Wallace Beery or Telly Savalas (Kojak on television) would look right armed with a monkey wrench or a piece of pipe. They would look right with a shotgun or a baseball bat. They would look absurd holding a fencing foil—and neither would know what to do with it. Cary Grant and David Niven have created scores of dashing characters in film who would look fine with a fencing foil or a neat revolver, but none of them would be able to cope with a length of lead pipe, a pool cue, or a bat. They could hold a shotgun, if it were a well crafted bird-hunting gun, and probably use it well. But if it were a sawed-off riot gun they would look wrong with it. Charl-

ton Heston looks right with almost any weapon in his hands. (In fact, I think he has done at least one "epic" film in every major historical period and has used virtually man's entire arsenal at one time or another.) By way of contrast, I cannot imagine Dick Van Dyke handling any weapon, from any period, well or willingly. In each case it is the nature of the man, something within his personality, that makes one kind of weapon right for him and another kind wrong.

If you think of these well-known actors as the characters they play (which they quite often are, type-casting being a reflex of the industry), the parallels involved in selecting weapons for the characters in your play become apparent. Often the playwright tells you what weapon the character is carrying, but much of the time he will say "a sword" or "a gun" and not specify what kind, what condition it is in, or how proficient the character is in its use.

Jack Cade, in Shakespeare's *Henry VI, Part II,* leads a commoner's rebellion and carries a sword. In fact, he is killed in a sword fight. But he is a commoner and as such was forbidden to own or carry a sword. The possession of one is part of his rebellion. That means, however, that his sword ought either to be old and rusty, a throwaway from a noble house, or a nobleman's sword in beautiful condition, having just been taken from the body of a murdered lord. In either case, he does not handle it well because he has never held one before. In choreographing his death scene, where he fights with a young knight and is easily overcome, he should try to use it as an impact weapon, beating at his opponent's sword as though he held a club, for that would be all he was used to fighting with. Cade's social status is defined in part, as is his personality, and his attitude, by the possession and use of that sword. The Earl of Warwick, by contrast, is a warrior by virtue of his being a healthy male in a noble household. That is one of the prime functions of his social class in 15th-century England. He is very proficient and quite at home with all weapons.

If the playwright tells you the character has "a gun," then it may be a pistol, a rifle, a shotgun, or a sub-machine gun. Which is right for your character? What caliber? What condition is it in? How well is it handled? You must decide these things based on the background of your character. If your man "has a knife," is it a jackknife, a hunting knife, a switchblade, or a butcher knife from the kitchen? Same problem: Who is he? How well does he handle it? The choice of weapon and the facility and familiarity with which it is handled speak volumes about the character you are trying to create for the audience. They can be among the most revealing things about him. Choose your weapon with care.

Gentlemen's Rules vs. Battlefield or Street Conditions

In dealing with combat situations on stage, you need to be aware of the difference between a formal match or contest between designated opponents, and a fight, which is a struggle for supremacy or even life itself. A contest is not a fight. It may employ combat techniques, but it is not a fight. A boxing match, a wrestling match (professional or amateur), a karate match, or a fencing match are all contests. There are definite times and signals to begin and to end the action. There are rules of conduct and limitations on the use of violence. The goal is to display superior skill, or to subdue your opponent through superior strength, or both. The designation of "winning by force" in boxing is to get your opponent down for ten seconds. In wrestling, it is to pin his shoulders to the mat for three seconds. A referee enforces both the time factors and the "rules of fair play."

Each contest has a definite line over which you cannot step in inflicting pain on your opponent. If you exceed this line grossly, the contest will be stopped and your opponent will be awarded the "win" because of a foul. The idea is always to display superiority, not to injure your opponent. The contest is over, theoretically, at any time the opponent cannot defend himself. In case of accidental injury to either party, the contest is stopped before further damage can be done. Violence is a definite factor. Brutality often enters in. However, as long as there are rules of "sportsmanship" and outside referees to enforce them, it is not a *fight*.

In team sports such as basketball, soccer, ice hockey, and particularly football, the same concept prevails. Football has been called "a controlled war." "Control" is the key word. Players may block and tackle each other in football; forechecking and backchecking in hockey are very physical. However, as soon as the physical contact in any of these games exceeds the carefully prescribed limits of the rules, a referee blows his whistle. Play stops and a penalty is assessed against the offender. Injury to any participant brings an immediate halt to play while the injured player is attended to. Team sports may simulate a battle. They have often been called a substitute for battle. They, themselves, are *not* a battle. Blood may flow and bones may crack, but this is sport, not war.

In all of the above, individual or team-oriented, "gentlemen's rules" prevail. The participants know the permissible bounds of action and largely stay within them. They may not know exactly what move to expect from an opponent, but they know the range of moves he is permitted, and they know what *not* to expect. Innovation and surprise within the rules is frequent and effective. Innovation outside the rules is occasional and is punished when detected.

On the battlefield, whether it be the field of Agincourt in Shakespeare's *Henry V;* a dusty street in Verona where Romeo, Mercutio, and Tybalt brawl; a back alley in New York's

Harlem where Rif, Tony, and Bernardo kill each other in *West Side Story;* or a gym in *Rally Round the Flag Boys,* in which a group of Army enlisted men and a bunch of local boys flail away at each other in a comic riot, the tactics and the rules are all the same: *anything goes!* It doesn't matter whether you are in individual combat—Prince Hal vs. Hotspur (*Henry IV, Part I*), Romeo vs. Tybalt (*Romeo and Juliet*), Eddie Carbone vs. Marco (*A View from the Bridge*)—or in group warfare: anything goes. Once the fight starts there is no weapon you cannot use and no limitation on the way you can use it.

Let us look at two concrete examples: *Hamlet* and *Henry IV, Part I.* In *Hamlet,* there is a duel between Hamlet and Laertes fought with rapier and dagger. The rapiers are supposed to be "bated" (or blunted), and it is supposed to be a contest of skill. It is to be scored on the basis of "touches," not wounds, the "touch" to be verified by Osric, who acts as judge. The duel will escalate into a fight at the last, but for our purposes let us look only at the first couple of "passes." This is strictly a contest in swordsmanship. All attacks and parries are initiated with the blades of the rapier and dagger. No other part of the weapon is used. No other part of the body is used. No additional weapon, such as a chair, stool, or cloak is employed. In that era, if either party had kicked or tripped the other, or enveloped his sword arm with a drapery or cloak, the contest would have been stopped and the aggressor severely censured for his unsportsmanlike conduct.

Henry IV, Part I, has both mass battle scenes and individual confrontations. I have seen several productions of this play and have performed in it. In my own production I staged the battles. Often, we had sixty actors flailing away at each other with a wide variety of swords, daggers, axes, maces, and spears. Although most of the "deaths" were accomplished with the business end of a weapon,

the majority of the decisive blows—the blows that disabled the opponent and made him helpless to resist the death stroke—were landed with the hilt of a sword, the butt of a spear, the edge of a shield, a helmet, a knee, a foot, a sharp elbow piece on the armor, etc. People were grabbed by the hair, the beard, the cloak, the collar, anything that was handy. On the battlefield or on the street there is no referee, there is no "time-out" (unless the combatants mutually agree to one), and there are no rules.

If any court swordsman, as opposed to a battle-tested nobleman (for example Osric, the court butterfly in *Hamlet,* or Laertes for that matter), ever got onto a battlefield with the Bloody Sergeant from *Macbeth* or the Earl of Warwick from *Henry VI,* they would last about five seconds. They would address their first opponent, say "En garde," and catch a foot in the crotch. Goodbye! If they managed to avoid the foot, they would still be in trouble. If, in the first exchange, they locked rapiers and daggers with their opponent, they would consider the moment a neutral standoff. While they leaned into the locked weapons and wrestled "properly" for advantage, their seasoned opponent would probably snap his wrists forward and bring his right elbow right across their respective jaws. Knockout . . . death! The battlefield is not a gymnasium. Do not confuse the two when planning your weapons handling.

As noted earlier, a person's choice and handling of a weapon are determined by his character. So too are his battle techniques. You can compress the essence of a character's personality and values into the few minutes of a long fight scene, even into the few seconds of a short one. A character may begin a battle scene with full awareness of the niceties and of ritual. As long as he is not severely challenged he may be gentlemanly, even chivalrous, sparing fallen foes, allowing an opponent to recover a lost weapon. If the fight is long and close, however, if life and/or honor is wholly at stake, then chivalry may begin to disappear.

In *Henry IV, Part I* the climactic confrontation is between Prince Hal and young Hotspur. The text of the play requires that Hal win, killing Hotspur. The structure of the play requires that he win by means acceptable to the audience, for he is to become Henry V, one of England's most popular kings. But in the first four acts of the play we have become very fond of Hotspur. We know him to be a superb warrior. The battle therefore needs to be long and desperate. It may start in a proper and chivalrous manner, with both men fully armed and fully confident. They are both experienced warriors, and so the tricks of full weapons use are theirs from the beginning. As the fight progresses weapons are lost or broken and others are snatched up from the fallen soldiers who preceded them on stage, or are improvised. Finally, through desperation and exhaustion the fight becomes elemental and animal. They tear at each other with hands, feet, teeth, and nails as well as weapons. A long and detailed staging of a possible climactic duel between Hal and Hotspur is included in Chapter XI of this book.

Essentially, what weapons handling comes down to is that under "gentlemen's rules" style and grace share the stage with skill; under "battlefield conditions," ancient or modern, stamina, ferocity, and pragmatism come into play and usually prevail. A given weapon can be used in many ways, including some not foreseen by its designer or manufacturer. Use your imagination.

Summary

In terms of safety, the most important section of this chapter is the first. The techniques of aiming and/or landing weapon blows against various parts of the anatomy are the first consideration in planning any stage fight. The importance here of kinesthetic learning, starting with slow motion and working slowly and carefully up to speed, is obvious. It should not need to be stressed again.

It must also be emphasized that in handling weapons from past eras, you are unlikely to be working with actual antiques. They are too valuable, too hard to find, and, you will probably find, too heavy for you to handle. Replicas of these weapons are available for purchase or rental from a wide variety of costume houses and also from specialty armory houses.[1] These replicas are designed for stage use. They duplicate the appearance of the authentic item but are lighter and more flexible. This is all to the good. I have worked with historically accurate replicas, constructed at two universities where I have taught and directed. Both the medieval sword of war and the 16th-century rapier are heavy! Unless you are in good shape they are difficult to control accurately and to manipulate with authority for any extended period of time. The lightweight stage versions will do nicely, provided only that the blades and guards are made of good metal and have a proper "ring" to them when they clash.

————

[1] See Appendix I.

Chapter VIII

SWORDS: TECHNIQUE AND APPLICATION FOR THE STAGE

Perhaps the first and most practical thing to say in this chapter is that I am not a fencer. I have had no formal training and have never held a sword in my hand outside of a theatre or a theatre classroom. That doesn't disturb me particularly.

In the professional theatre there are a number of fine actors with classical training who have studied fencing. They are at least proficient, and perhaps expert, in the handling of swords, and they are a distinct minority among their professional peers. There are virtually no actors on the amateur level of civic, community, university, college, high-school, or children's theatres who have had fencing training and/or competition experience. Yet if we work in the theatre for any length of time, many or most of us, in one production or another, will have to handle a sword on stage. I have learned to handle swords by working enough with expert fencers to determine which of their techniques apply to the stage and which are unnecessary or unworkable for our purposes in the creation of illusion. There are relatively few genuine fencing techniques that you must actually learn in order to create the impression of competency on the stage, and there are numerous delicate and very effective fencing maneuvers that would be of no use to learn because they could not be seen more than ten feet away. We will concern ourselves in this chapter with those facets and factors of sword handling that can be easily learned and can create tremendous excitement in the audience without necessitating a trip to the hospital emergency room.

DANGER: FLYING STEEL

Before we go further, a word about the dangers inherent in stage swordplay. There are two basic categories of danger: danger to those who *do* know how to fence, and danger to those novices who do not know sword handling.

In the former case we often have exuberance and the confidence of genuine skill substituting for planning and common sense. Laurence Olivier is hardly an unknown or untrained actor. Yet he has been injured many times and has caused many an injury for the very reason that he is an expert swordsman. In the introduction to a book by William Hobbs,[1] Olivier describes a production of *Romeo and Juliet* in which he was playing Mercutio. In one performance he virtually severed Tybalt's thumb. The next night he found himself facing an understudy in the role who was fierce, probably rather frightened by his predecessor's fate, and an expert swordsman in his own right. Using bucklers (small shields) and hand-and-a-half broadswords, they went at each other with sufficient zeal, wrote Olivier, that "no holds were barred and sparks flew like Japanese crackers and it was more up to the audience to defend itself as best it could rather than either of us." Olivier is delighted to note that almost every night of that production a piece of someone's sword

---

[1] Hobbs, William. *Stage Fight.* New York: Theatre Arts Books, 1967, p. 6.

89

snapped off under the pressure of combat and went zinging out into the audience. He also announces, with some pride, the possession of "untold slashes including a full thrust razor-edged sword wound in the breast." With all due respect for Lord Olivier's brilliance as a performer, I think he is foolhardy. The above-mentioned Tybalt (Geoffry Toone) may have his doubts as well, and I rather imagine that I would get a vote of agreement from those members of his audience who caught flying pieces of jagged steel during the course of a performance.

The major danger for trained swordsmen comes when they do not choreograph the fight, but merely "go at each other" until it is time for the designated character to "win the battle." They are relying on each other's skills and reflexes to an appalling degree. It is sad but true that on several occasions actors have been run through and killed because they weren't quite as quick or as skilled as they and/or their partners thought they were. At least a professional actor knows what he is doing. He knows, or certainly ought to, what the inherent risks are in "free-form" sword-play. He is doing this for a living, and he can make an informed decision that he does or does not care to take the risk. With or without the presence of "informed consent," it is my earnest recommendation that professional actors never "free-form" a sword fight. Choreograph it to the last detail.

When we come to the amateur actor (or a professional without fencing training), we are in a whole different world. There is a tendency to trust the director in all areas, rather than merely in those areas where he has demonstrated expertise. The notion abounds that "if good old Hank says that's the way to do it, then that's what we ought to do." This is especially prevalent in academic theatre, where a director's displeasure with an actor can be swiftly translated into a failing grade in what is supposed to be an unrelated course. The director may know a great deal about other aspects of theatre without knowing anything about swords. I must assume that all directors have the intelligence not to suggest, and the decency not to coerce, their actors into "working it out somehow" or "free-forming" any fight at all, and particularly one with weapons. Where this assumption proves groundless I must then turn to the actors and suggest that they politely sheathe and/or encase their weapons, place them carefully on the properties table, and refuse to touch them again.

What do we do when goodwill and common sense are in plentiful supply on all sides, but no one knows how to handle swords? Read on! Work with the suggestions in this book. Work it out together carefully, slowly, step by step, in choreography. You can achieve a good-looking sword fight, with safety, if you employ the same care and detailed preparation that we talked about with hand-to-hand combat. The more you know about swordplay when you start, the better it will look; of course, that is true. But it is not awkwardness that will kill or injure an actor; it is carelessness. When weapons are in use, there is no place for improvisation in the theatre.

There is, in addition, the danger that comes from horseplay. There is an almost universal tendency—and not only among the young—for an actor to metamorphose into Errol Flynn the moment he gets a sword in his hand. As soon as the swords are delivered from the costume shop, rental agency, metal workshop, or wherever, eager hands grab for them and otherwise sensible young (and not so young) men start yelling "En garde" at each other and swashing and buckling all over the rehearsal area. The risks attendant on this activity are obvious. One can call this kind of behavior infantile and stupid. The fact is, however, that the urge is constant. It transcends all barriers of age, sex, education, and experience. The only difference is that the experienced sword handler knows better, and controls himself. Perhaps, then, the best thing to do in the situation is to be aware that the urge will be there.

Accept the fact of it. Talk about it beforehand. Then resist the temptation at all costs and with iron discipline!

All of the suggestions, rules, and procedures for the safe handling of weapons given in Chapters VI and VII are obviously applicable here. If you have any doubts about this, I suggest two experiments to you, both undertaken with appropriate safeguards.

First, take your weapon and place the handle or butt of it on the ground. Making sure that a) there is no one around to bump into you; b) that your own footing is secure; and c) that your balance is secure, place the upturned blunted point of the weapon against your abdomen. Slowly and gradually increase the weight you allow to rest on the point. You will realize frighteningly soon how little of your weight is needed before you fully believe that the weapon will penetrate your body if you fall on it.

Second, take the weapon and—assuring items a, b, and c above for security's sake, hold the handle of it at arm's length and very lightly and carefully touch the tip to your eye socket. Please notice that the point or tip of almost any sword-type weapon ever made will fit into the eye socket, given any impetus at all.

Do not carry, handle, or utilize these weapons carelessly or thoughtlessly. A foil tucked under your arm is a potentially lethal "stinger" if you simply turn to answer a question, trailing the blade in an arc behind you. It is pathetically easy for another actor on stage, backstage, or on the stairs behind you to walk or fall into the blade.

Swords were originally created and designed for the purpose of killing people. They are still quite capable of doing that. Handle with care!

THE DIFFERENCE BETWEEN COMPETITION FENCING AND STAGE FENCING

Amateur and Olympic fencing use primarily foil, rapier, and saber. All are thrusting weapons. The rapier and saber can also be employed as cutting weapons. In each case the weapons are extremely light and flexible. Particularly the foil and rapier can be moved, and are moved, with a lightning quick snap of the wrist and fingers. With the foil, thrust and parry are "inside maneuvers." That is, the defender keeps the attacker's blade to the outside of his body by keeping his defensive blade between the attacker's blade and his own body. A move of 2 or 3 inches accomplished by a rotation of the wrist is enough to free up the attacker's blade and to present a threat that must be immediately countered or the match is lost. The countering move by the defender is often a corresponding 2- or 3-inch rotation of the wrist. This move forms a barrier that the attacker's blade cannot penetrate, and so the attacking blade slides past its target. Both fencers are in superb condition, as fencing is one of the most physically demanding of sports. They are both on balance, every muscle tensed, every nerve alert for an opening. It all should be very exciting and very dramatic. To those who know and understand fencing, it is. To those of us who are uninformed and do not know what to look for, however, it is baffling and dull. This is because the moves are so quick and small that they cannot be seen from any distance. Obviously we can see the lunges, for they are large movements. Everything else is likely to escape us. The dramatic weakness of this situation is manifest. Foil and rapier technique cannot be used to good effect on a stage because the strokes and parries are not large enough. Though it may make a fencing buff shudder, we should use saber technique, or its equivalent, at all times, regardless of its historical inappropriateness with the weapon in hand.

Saber technique allows both stabbing and slashing/cutting. The attacking strokes and the defensive counterstrokes are all large "outside" blows involving at minimum the whole arm and shoulder, and preferably the whole body. A preparatory backswing and/or the engagement of the entire body in the effort of the blow is dramatically desirable. While thrusting-stabbing motions and countermoves are part of this choreography, they are used infrequently. The majority of moves are full-body cutting motions. The counterparries are full-body sword actions as well. They are large. They are visible. They are flashy. They are relatively safe, when done correctly.

Of course, these outside strokes are artificial in that no sane combatant on the battlefield, the amateur mat, or the street corner would ever take a wide outside cut with a stabbing weapon. The moment he did so, any alert opponent would thrust straight in and pass his weapon right through the idiot's unprotected body. The point is that we are not in any of those places. We are on a stage, and both stroke and parry have been choreographed. Just as life cannot be art until accurate history is selected, structured, and reordered to a pleasing aesthetic harmony of character, action, and dialogue, so swordplay cannot be dramatically artistic until it has been so selected, structured, and reordered. By going to large, outside sword movement, regardless of the nature of the weapon employed, we are going to convey a strong, realistic and visible impression of weapons handling to our audience.

Note: In some cases the whole body can be engaged in one direction, to swing the weapon as rapidly and as hard as you can. (See the section on Offensive and Defensive Arcs, below.) In most cases, however, isometrics is an integral part of the choreography. You create the illusion of ultimate violence by employing every muscle in your body. But, by employing them isometrically you control your blade velocity and torque, thereby providing an additional margin for error.

STANCE AND POSITION

As with all other aspects of stage violence the primary mechanics of sword work is maintaining your balance. Different weapons will demand or suggest different movement patterns according to their length, weight, and maneuverability and also according to their function as thrusting or cutting weapons. In this segment we will be concerned with: 1) body positions, when you are at rest but on guard waiting for an opening; 2) hand position, how you grip the sword to best advantage; and 3) foot positions, again, when you are at rest and waiting for an opening. These are called "guards."

Body positions

There are two basic positions. If you are holding both an offensive and a defensive weapon, such as sword and shield, or rapier and dagger, or sword and cloak, then both hands are involved in the combat. In this case your body position is square to your opponent. You are face to face, and this stance is common up through the 16th century. If you are dealing with one weapon only which must be used for both offense and defense, there is a tendency to stand sideways to each other, exposing only your side to your opponent. By the late 17th century, the rapier was the premier weapon, and the use of the left hand for defense was almost unknown. An occasional disarm was attempted by grasping the opponent's blade with a heavily gauntleted left hand and pulling it free. This was rare, however, and the left hand was out of the picture except as an aid to balance. Therefore the duelist held the rapier extended in his right hand, point toward his opponent, and kept the rest of his body as far out of "the line of fire" as possible.

The obvious exception to this rule of thumb is the two-hand broadsword, which is used alone, without shield, dagger, or cloak. Both hands are grasping the sword. This weapon can be used to stab, but its primary action is as a cutting and impact weapon. In handling a broadsword, one would assume a square-on position.

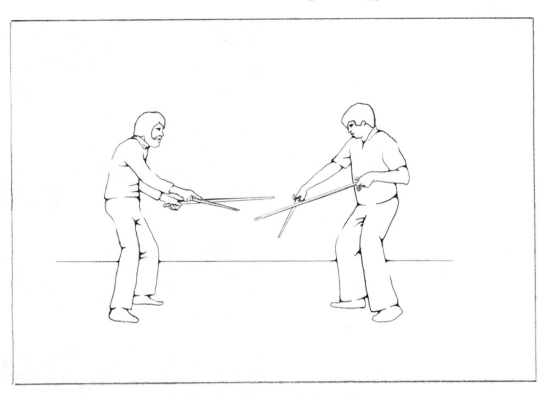

Figure 35 *Square-on body position*

Figure 36 *Side-to-side body position*

Hand grip

There are two basic grips to use with a sword, and the one you choose will depend on your own hand and wrist strength in relationship to the weight of the weapon. The preferred grip is to lay your thumb on top of the sword handle, curl the second joint of the index finger under the handle, and then hold the sword in place by pressing the handle lightly and diagonally into your palm with the first digit of the remaining three fingers. This is a light and flexible grip. It gives you maximum flexibility of maneuver with your hand and wrist to control the blade. It is analagous to the nature and function of the correct knife grip described in Chapter VI. Do not curl your fingers completely around the handle. Do not grip the blade tightly at all times. When you and your opponent are feinting or "testing" each other with light taps of the blade, there is no need to tighten the grip at all. As the blades clash with greater velocity and ferocity, you should tighten the grip proportionally as the blades come together. You would also tighten your grip as you made an offensive thrust. Please note that I said "tighten" the grip, not change it. There is no need to curl your fingers completely around the handle. You tighten the grip of the curled index finger and increase the pressure of your thumb on the top of the blade and of the first digit of the remaining fingers, thus increasing the "vise-grip" of the handle against your palm. That should be sufficient. This light grip will work for any sword weapon you are strong enough to maneuver that way.

That said, we will all find plenty of swords we are not strong enough to handle that way. Only a lumberjack could love a "sword-of-war." This is a hand-and-a-half weapon, meaning it was designed to be used with either one hand or two, depending on whether or not you had a shield. It was roughly 36 inches long and 2 inches wide and weighed about 8 pounds. This weapon was not handled with a light grip. The only way to control it was to wrap your fingers around the handle as tightly

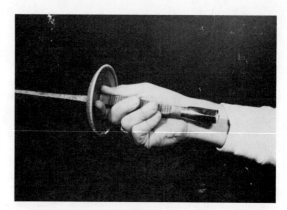

Figure 37   *Light sword grip*

Figure 38   *Heavy sword grip*

as possible and wrap your thumb around your fingers in an overlapping grip. Power to cut or crush an opponent through his armor, not quickness, was the long suit of this weapon. While the overlapping grip is necessary with the broadsword (one-and-a-half or two-hand variety), it is always an option for use with any sword you cannot control with the light grip described above. The simplest rule of thumb is that if you cannot control the blade and make it go consistently where you want it to with the light grip, then use the overlapping grip instead. The need to maintain control of your blade as a safety factor overrides any and all other considerations.

Foot positions

Through the 16th century the square-on body position is dominant, and there are three basic foot positions, or "guards." They correspond to the business at hand: "attack," "defense," and "neutral." In each case you are doing the same thing. You are maintaining your center of balance as you await or pursue your next choreographed action. A "guard" is a launching pad. It is the position from which you make your next move, not the position you wind up in. After an offensive flurry, for example, which has not concluded the fight and which has evolved into a pause, you would assume your next guard, according to your expectation of what is going to happen next. In all three guards, the feet are spread comfortably for balance, at roughly shoulder width. The weight is on the balls of the feet. The knees are slightly bent, for balance.

In a neutral guard, the feet are level with each other, and you are ready to move in any direction that circumstances dictate. Your weapons are held at roughly waist level, a little way out from the body, also ready for either attack or defense, whichever seems appropriate.

In an attack guard your right foot is slightly in advance of your left and your sword arm is extended toward some portion of your opponent's body. The left arm, holding shield, dagger, or cloak—whatever defensive weapon you have—is pulled in tight to your body, ready to ward off any counterattack.

In a defensive guard, you withdraw your right foot slightly behind your left. The defensive weapon is extended toward the opponent to ward off the expected blow, and the weapon in the right hand is held in close to the body, point toward the opponent in preparation for a counterthrust should the opening present itself.

As the rapier became lighter and more flexible in the 17th century and the one-handed fight came into vogue, the side-to-side body

Figure 39 *Foot position—neutral guard, square-on*

Figure 40 *Foot position—attack guard, square-on*

position took hold. In this circumstance the combatants start by standing sideways to each other, with their right sides toward each other. They are more than arm and sword's length apart so that neither can hit the other merely by extending his arm. Each assumes a guard with his feet roughly shoulder width apart; their knees are slightly bent for balance, and they are on the balls of their feet. The feet are at roughly right angles; that is, the right toe is pointing at the opponent, ready to stride forward or back as the tide of battle ebbs and flows. The left foot has the toe pointing straight out from the belt buckle.

With righthanded combatants, both advancing and retreating strides are led with the right foot, and the left foot supports the stride by following it up and reestablishing the guard. If "A" has an advantage and is pressing his opponent back, he will stride forward, let us say, 14 inches with his right foot. He will then

Figure 41 *Foot position—defensive guard, square-on*

Figure 42 *Foot position—side-by-side position*

bring his left foot up 14 inches and reestablish his guard in the same proportion and balance he had originally. "B's" retreat would be the same in reverse: right foot back 14 inches, then left foot back 14 inches to reestablish the guard and keep his balance.

There is a move in rapier fighting called "the pass." From the offensive guard, it is tricky and dangerous. If it doesn't work you're

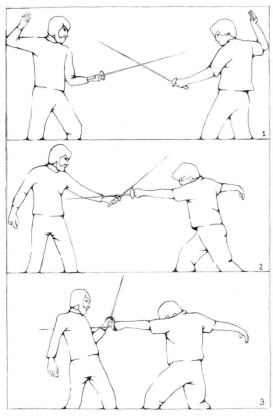

Figure 43   "The Pass"

likely to wind up as the one receiving the wound instead of dealing it out. From the defensive guard it is a little safer, but it still has risks. Instead of advancing 14 inches with the front foot, bringing up the rear for support and lunging, "A" will "pass" his rear foot in front of the other; then he extends his original lead foot as far as he can, perhaps 24 to 30 inches, and lunges. He bends his forward knee for flexibility and pushes as far off a straight-

ened rear leg as he can. "A" is now very far extended and way off balance. He has probably had to use his hand, on the floor, to keep his balance at all. If "B" tried to escape the lunge by backpedaling, he probably didn't make it and has been pierced by the lunge. If he saw the "pass" coming and sidestepped it, however, "B" is in much better shape than "A." "B" is on his feet, on guard, and on balance. "A" is half on the floor, practically spreadeagled and completely off balance. It is highly unlikely that he can recover in time to ward off a counterattack. "B" can score a hit practically at will. You should use a "pass" off an offensive guard in your choreography only when you want one or the other of your combatants to score a hit. The result will likely be the same off a defensive guard. It is a climactic, or subclimactic, move.

CUT, THRUST, AND PARRY

Thus far we've talked about how you hold your body, how you position your feet, and how you grip the sword. Now, how do you wield it? Let's divide this section into three categories: 1) rules of the road; 2) attacking maneuvers; and 3) defensive maneuvers.

Rules of the road

No matter which type of sword you are dealing with, there are certain rules you must follow for reasons of both aesthetics and safety:

a) When a cut is supposed to be successfully parried, always aim at the portion of the opponent's anatomy you are supposed to be swinging at. Do not plan the cut to miss. First of all, it looks terrible. A blow aimed at the opponent's shield or sword blade will create no illusion. It looks like what it is, a fake. Second, a cut aimed to one side of your opponent, instead of at him, is harder to parry successfully without making your partner overreach his balance. Because he is more off balance, he is more likely to misplay this beat of the fight and/or the following beat (which may be aimed at *you*), and you are increasing the danger of an accident. Therefore, you endanger your partner and yourself by swinging to miss, whatever your good intentions. You do not protect him.

b) Do not plan a cut to land on the body of your opponent, even if he is wearing armor. Remember that costume armor is most likely made of celastic, or some kind of plastic. It might be made of light metal, painted and trimmed to look like steel, but a heavy blade, swung with realistic force, is likely to go right through it. Even if you successfully employ isometrics so that the blade ricochets off the armor in a "realistic" manner, the sound you get will be that of steel on plastic or tin. It will be hollow and illusion-shattering. The scene will be hurt even if your partner is not.

It is not necessary to take the aesthetic and personal risks that come with landing your blade on your opponent's body or limbs. You can use the power and force of a cut on his blade or shield to "beat him to his knees" or "throw him off balance." You can then "finish him off" with a thrust in the next phase of the fight. Remember, in all such cases, that the receiving actor controls his own balance, just as in the procedures of unarmed combat.

c) Lethal or disabling wounds should be "inflicted" with a thrust action. These, of course, pass by the body or limb of the actor, not through. The "passing-by" will follow earlier suggestions and either go upstage of the actor or, in arena, be a fast "in and out," masked as much as possible.

d) A thrust to be caught on a shield, or parried by the defensive action of your opponent, should always be *at* the target, not away or completely to one side of it, for the same reasons as noted above in "a." There is one modification, and one precaution.

The modification is that thrusts need not be aimed at the center of the body. If aimed off-center, at a shoulder, or side, it is both easier

and safer to deflect them with a proper parry.

The precaution is that all thrusting motions should be restricted to the area well below the face and neck. Aim for the pectoral muscles and below. Never aim higher than that. The face and neck are just too vulnerable to admit of any error. A combination of the blunted tip of the weapon, isometric control of the lunge, and practice to the point of kinesthetic security will provide your safety factors here. The worst that should be sustained in case of error is a bruise, and even that shouldn't happen if you have practiced the exchange to the point where it is reflexive.

e) When the blades meet, they should always meet at a right angle (90°). This is for maximum effect and security. You may plan to meet at 90 degrees and be slightly off. Then the blades might meet at 60 or 70 degrees. In that case the "meet" will still hold and the blades will clash in a secure manner. If you plan for a meeting at a 45- to 60-degree angle, and you are off, then the blades come together at such an oblique angle that they will slide right off of each other. If that happens it will look foolish. Worse, if that happens you do not know where the blades are going to wind up as you follow through your swing. They may slither off each other onto or into an actor. Try to make them come together at an angle of 90 degrees!

f) When the blades meet, they should always meet at the approximate center of the respective blades. Again, this is both for maximum sound effect and for security. If you plan to meet at the center of the blades and you are off by 6 to 9 inches, you are still all right. If you plan to meet with the center of one blade striking the other near the handle, and you are off by 6 to 9 inches, your opponent may lose a thumb. An error in the other direction, toward the far end of the blade, will not cause an injury (although it might cause the tip of one of the weapons to break off and become a flying missile), but it will neither look nor sound very convincing to your audience.

Figure 44 *Proper angle and position of a weapons clash*

g) Always handle a cut, thrust, or parry with the "sharp" edge of your sword, not the flat width of it. It looks better and sounds better. You have better control of your blade when you do so, because the grip on your weapon was designed for you to maneuver the blade in that way.

Attacking maneuvers

Attacking maneuvers can be divided into cuts, thrusts, and punches:

a) Cuts

Cuts usually come out of the "attacking guard," although they can be used as a defensive maneuver, as well, which was described earlier in the chapter. Your right foot strides past your left and, with isometric control restraining the actual velocity of the full bodily effort, you swing the blade with your whole body supporting your right arm and shoulder.

It is somewhat like handling a tennis racket. You can come straight overhand at the head. You can come three-quarter forearm overhand at the upper-left quadrant of your partner. You can come side-arm forehand at his waist, and by bending and flexing your own knees, you can come side-arm forehand at his legs.

If you turn your wrist over you can come three-quarter backhand at his upper right quadrant; side-arm backhand at his right side and waist; and by bending and flexing your own knees, you can come side-arm backhand at his legs. The single, and vital, difference between a tennis backhand stroke and a sword-arm backhand stroke is in the position of the wrist. With a tennis-racket backhand, you have the back of your hand and wrist toward the net and your opponent as you pull your arm through the stroke. To achieve this, as you pull your racket over from forehand to backhand, you turn your palm toward your body, and your thumb comes up as it grips the handle. With a sword, you turn your palm and knuckles out, toward your opponent, as you start your stroke, and your thumb is down, at the bottom of the grip. In this way, you are presenting the sharpened cutting edge of your blade to your opponent, not the back.

When blows are aimed at the area of the knee, or below, try to keep the blade parallel to the ground. It will prevent your accidentally slamming the tip of your sword into the stage floor.

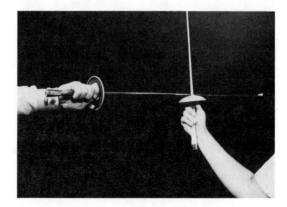

Figure 45 *Sword grip for a backhand cut*

b) Thrusts

Not all sword weapons were meant for thrusting. For example, the broadsword was primarily a cutting and impact weapon. However, virtually all swords had some kind of sharp point and could be used for that purpose. A thrust can be an attack, a feint, or a counterattack, and can thus be launched from any of the three guards. It can consist of an extension of the sword arm, with no body follow-through whatever. It can be a full-fledged lunge, or even a "pass" as described earlier in this chapter in the section on foot positions.

When a thrust is defensive, an attempt to discourage, ward off, or deflect an attack, the body is in a neutral or defensive guard. Only the arm and shoulder are employed, and there is not much force.

When a thrust is an offensive action, it comes out of either a neutral or an offensive guard. When both hands are engaged, the right foot strides past the left, the right knee is flexed to lengthen the reach, and the left leg straightens and "pushes off" to add strength and velocity to the thrust.

In the 17th century and later, when only one weapon, in one hand, was employed in combat, the side-to-side body position was employed. In this case a lunge is a full extension of the right arm, supported by a stride with the right foot and a lunging of the body. The assailant must be careful not to extend his stride so far as to be off balance, for if his opponent parries or sidesteps the lunge, the assailant needs to be able to withdraw to his guard just as quickly as he lunged. If he cannot, if he is overextended, he is in trouble.

Before employing any thrusts in your choreography, please reread the rules of the road given earlier in this chapter, and follow them carefully. To be on the receiving end of a thrust is a dangerous maneuver for the actor who is an experienced swordsman. For the novice it is a potential disaster. Use it carefully and sparingly.

c) Punches

As noted in the section on Gentleman's Rules vs. Battlefield or Street Conditions, the hand guard, knuckle-bow, pommel, or hilt of a sword are just as much weapons as the blade. If you close with your opponent, you can use the hilt of your sword as an effective weapon to set up the killing thrust that will follow. If you wish to use these techniques, go back to Chapters III and IV on Body Blows and Head Blows, and follow those procedures.

There is one addition, however. When using the hilt of a sword for a weapon, be sure the blade is to one side of, between, and/or parallel to you and your partner, and clear of all bodies in the immediate vicinity. It will not do much for your safety record to get a beautiful punch to the jaw of your opponent with your right fist wrapped around the handle of your sword—and at the same time inadvertently stab an actor fighting someone else two feet upstage of you.

Defensive maneuvers

Defensive maneuvers also break down into two categories: a) parrying with a shield designed for that specific purpose, or with a makeshift shield such as a barrel lid, a stool, or a chair light enough to wield with one hand; and b) parrying with a blade. The basic techniques are the same whether you are using a dagger in your left hand in two-hand (two-weapon) combat or whether you are using a sword or rapier in your right hand in one-weapon combat.

One can, of course, use a cloak, drape, tablecloth, or other piece of heavy fabric for defense. In this case, however, it can be used only to entangle or otherwise deflect a thrust away from your body. It is of little or no use against a cut or punch, except to muffle the impact and reduce the damage that would otherwise be inflicted. If your opponent is using a heavy weapon such as a broadsword,

Figure 46   *Parrying with a shield*

the weight and velocity of the blade would smash right through the cloth. A lighter weapon, such as a rapier or saber, would not have the same weight and power behind the blow. It would, however, be theoretically sharper, and because of its relative lightness it would develop enough torque and velocity to cut through the cloth. For these reasons, you cannot really convince an audience that a cut or slash was stopped by cloth, even if the two of you do stop the blade with isometrics.

a) Parrying with a shield

The handling of a shield for defensive purposes is rather simple and obvious: get it in front of the blow!

1) Make sure that the blow to be parried lands at, or near, the center of the shield. This provides you with the maximum margin for error should the assailant's blow be slightly off target.

2) Try to have the blade meet the shield at as close to a right angle as you can. It diminishes the chances of the assailant's blade glancing off, or ricocheting off the shield and going out of control on the follow-through.

3) Grip your shield tightly and have your left forearm firmly buttressed against the inside of it when the blow lands. Otherwise you may have it torn out of your hand by the impact of the blow, or you may have it driven back hard enough into the back of your hand and your forearm to cause discomfort. Bruises aren't lethal, or even disabling most of the time, but why absorb any unnecessary discomfort?

4) If you are receiving a blow from a heavy weapon, get your shield arm in close to your body, with your elbow and shoulder locked and tensed, so that your whole body is leaning into the blow and helping to absorb it. An aggressive blow with little power behind it, either because of the weight of the weapon or

Figure 47 *Parrying with a blade: overhead parry*

the condition of the aggressor, can be picked off with the shield arm alone. A heavy blow cannot be handled that way. Your whole body needs to support the defensive maneuver.

b) Parrying with a blade

Parrying is a little more complicated with a blade. Cuts and thrusts are parried in different ways.

Cuts

1) An overhead blow is parried by getting your blade up, over, and out in front of your head, with your blade parallel to the floor. Your arm will be extended to its full length to keep the attacking blade as far from you as possible. Your hand position will vary with the length of your blade, but the idea is always for the center of his blade to meet the center of yours. Assuming that your opponent is

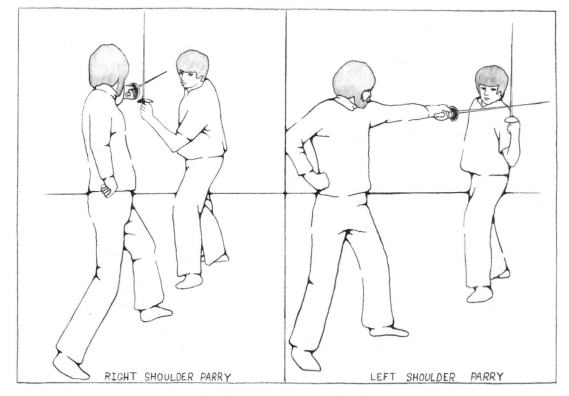

RIGHT SHOULDER PARRY   LEFT SHOULDER PARRY

Figure 48 *Parrying with a blade: shoulder parry*

attempting to land straight down on top of your head on a line with your nose, then the center of your blade should be on a line with the bridge of your nose as well. A dagger, in your left hand, might wind up with the handle (and your hand) on a line with or just outside of your left ear in order to accomplish this. A sword some 36 inches long, in your right hand, might wind up with the handle (and your hand) on a line with or just outside of your right shoulder. The point of contact is what is important, and that is the center of your blade. As you go through this maneuver in *painfully* slow motion it will become immediately apparent to both you and your partner why he must aim his blade exactly where you both agreed it would go—the center of your forehead. If he tries to "protect" you by sliding off to one side or another so as to avoid the more vulnerable head area, he will come down on your unprotected hand or your unprotected shoulder, depending on which way he "cheated" the blow.

2) A shoulder parry is achieved by thrusting the arm out almost to its full length with the blade vertical to the floor. In dealing with a blow to the left shoulder which you are parrying with a dagger in your left hand or with a sword in your right hand (one-hand combat), extend the arm as far as you can to keep the blade out away from you. In a right shoulder parry you would probably use your sword, whether you had a dagger in your left hand or not. An opponent coming at you backhand, as he swings at your right shoulder, is moving his blade in an arc that is closer to your body than it would be in a forehand blow. Therefore you may need to get your right arm and elbow bent somewhat (and closer to your body) to intercept the arc of his swing.

The sword is vertical to the floor, point up, and the center of your blade should cover the area of his target so that a "mid-blade meet" is the result. The process is the same for left-handed fencers.

3) "Flank" or waist and leg parries in-

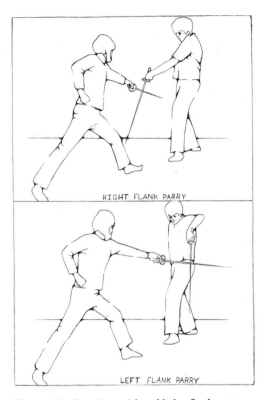

Figure 49 *Parrying with a blade: flank parry*

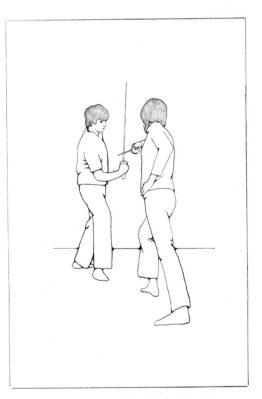

Figure 50 *Parrying with a blade: "gate" parry*

volve getting the center of your blade to cover the target area, with the blade held either vertically to the floor (point down) or diagonally, with the handle at, or slightly above, waist height. The point should be sloping downward. The angle at which you hold the blade will be determined by the target you are defending, as you are setting up a situation in which the blades will meet in the center of each and at 90 degrees to each other. The angle at which he attacks will determine the angle at which you parry. As this will never be a surprise to either of you (it had better not be!), you can plan the angles that will be most comfortable and most effective for you.

Thrusts

One can parry a thrust with what is called a "circular parry." Those of you who are sufficiently experienced in swordplay to manage this maneuver safely don't need this section of my book anyway. For the novice, it is just too dangerous. Don't try it. The best you can do is look inept. It's all downhill to surgery from there!

The basic technique of parrying a thrust is to set up a "gate" that the opponent's blade cannot get through.

1) Hold your blade perpendicular to the attacking blade. Your opponent's blade will be more or less parallel to the floor when he thrusts, depending on his height relationship to you. (Is he on a step above or below you? Is he on one knee? etc.) Your blade will be more or less vertical to the floor. If his target is below the waist, your blade will be point down. If his target is above the waist, your blade will be point up.

2) If you remember the rules of the road earlier in this chapter, you will realize that the thrust is not coming at the center of your body. It is headed for your right or left side. Extend your arm in front of you. Catch his blade with yours and "force" it to travel outside of your blade on a path that takes it outside of your body target area. Once you have engaged his horizontal point with your vertical blade, your opponent continues his thrust and his blade cannot get past the "gate." It has to travel past you instead of through you. It can slide the entire length of the attacking blade, riding along past the center of the defensive blade.

3) You and your partner can end the thrust wherever you wish. Once the parry is firm he can withdraw after only 12 inches of his blade has slid past (but not through) your guard. He can commit himself fully to the lunge and run a full 3 feet of steel along your defensive blade, fetching up when the hilt clangs against your weapon (that makes a lovely sound!). You can come out of that maneuver anywhere in between those extremes that you wish. Once the gate is set up, and the assailant's tip is caught and pushed outside, you are perfectly safe. He can't put that blade into you no matter how hard he lunges.

4) A variation on this is the "beat." It is essentially the same as Steps 1 through 3 above, except that in Step 2 you slap or "beat" your opponent's blade to the outside with an extra snap of your wrist and arm, instead of merely extending the defensive weapon in time to set up a stationary gate. The beat works as well as the gate and is more appropriate against heavier types of swords.

DISARMS

There are numerous disarms that derive from wrestling and unarmed martial arts. For these, see Chapter V. In addition, one can disarm with a cloak or other piece of cloth, or by grabbing an opponent's blade with a well-gloved hand and pulling it loose. What I am concerned with here is solely the technique of taking control of an opponent's blade with your own.

After parrying a cut or thrust, the person parrying starts moving his blade in an arc that

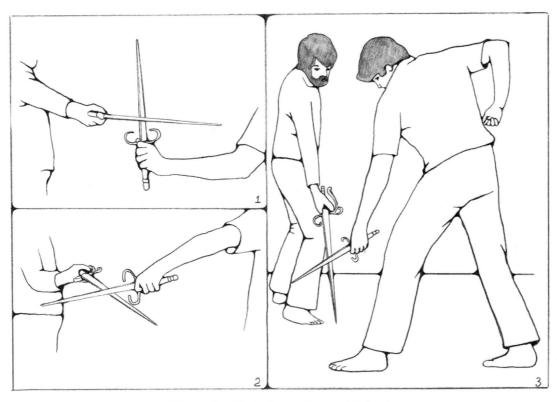

Figure 51 *Blade disarm: dagger, left hand*

forces the opponent's blade to travel in front of it. You can either:

1) Maneuver your blade with an inside circular movement, so that your blade (which has been inside of or under the attacking blade, forcing it away from you) has now circled it and is outside and/or above the attacking blade. You then force the blade down on to the floor and step on the end of it. Your opponent's blade is now immobile, and he must release it and move back to escape your blade.

For example, if you have a left-hand parry on a left shoulder cut with your dagger, then your dagger is vertical, point up, and inside of the attacking blade, which is horizontal. Simply step in with your left foot to gain leverage, roll your blade over the top of the attacking blade, and lean down on it. It has to go down if he has not withdrawn it in time. Force his blade to the floor, step on it, and you have him.

Let us say you have a left flank parry with a sword in your right hand because you are in a one-weapon combat situation. Your opponent's sword is at waist level, parallel to the floor once the parry is made, no matter whether he attacked with a cut or a thrust. Your right arm is extended across your body. Your blade is vertical, point down, blocking his blade. As you are in a side-to-side body position, your right foot is already advanced in front of your left. Take a heel-toe pivot to your left, with your right foot remaining as it is. (If you need to close with him more, then slide your right foot forward into him and bring up your left foot for balance before pivoting, all the while holding the parry.) You now have your back pressed into his front, and the parry is still held as it was. Roll your blade over the top of his blade and force it downward to the floor. Step on it. Push him off with your body or your left elbow. He has to let go.

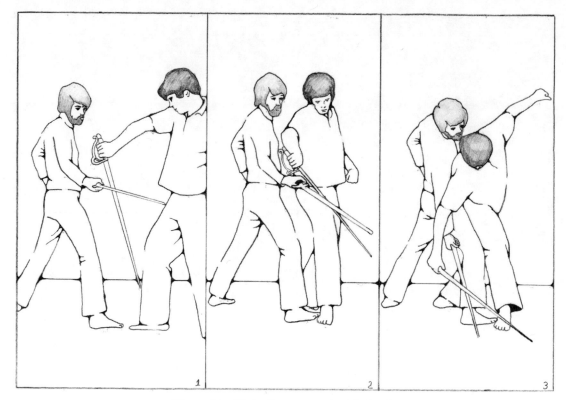

Figure 52 *Blade disarm: sword, right hand*

The variations are numerous depending on the types of swords, the relative size and weight of the combatants, and their stage positions. The principle remains constant. The defensive blade maneuvers over on top of the offensive blade either by rolling over in constant contact or by letting go of contact for a split second to circle inside of and over it. Once the defensive blade is on top, it presses the attacking blade down into the floor. In each case the attacker's blade is stopped by a parry—a reversal of blade position is achieved by the defender—and the attacker's blade is forced straight down to the floor.

2) You can also achieve a disarm by main force. Having achieved the parry, you simply force the attacker's blade back with your own, whipping it over his head and down to the floor on the other side.

If you are in a left flank parry, similar to the one above, your blade is pointed down and his is parallel to the floor. Curl your blade slightly under his so that the pressure you are bringing to bear is up instead of out. Whip his blade upward and continue to curl yours under his, so that when the blades are head high you are starting to force his blade to your right and to his left. Continue the whipping motion. By now your blade is pointing straight up; his is still more or less parallel to the floor. Continue the motion and your blade comes over on top of his so that at shoulder level both blades are parallel to the floor. As you reach this point you have pivoted your body and arm to the left, so that with your arm extended the two blades are at right angles. He has been forced by the pressure to pivot slightly to his left, but his blade is still pointing to approximately where your body *was*. Your point has pivoted almost 90 degrees *to your right*. You now have complete control of his blade. Continue the motion and force his blade to the floor. Step on it! Done!

I have described this in stages to make the

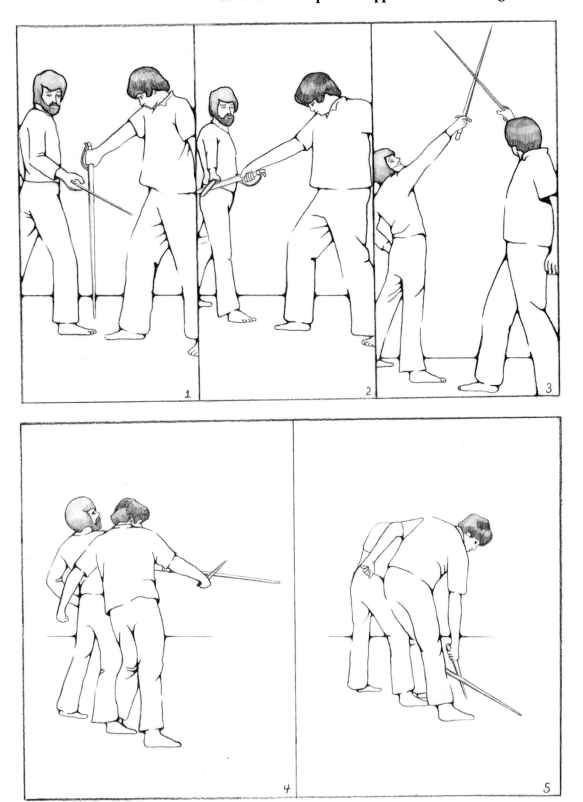

Figures 53 and 54 *Blade disarms: sword, right hand*

Figure 55   *Blade disarm: sword, right hand*

sequence of the action clear. When you practice it initially, do practice it in those stages. However, the finished product should be one long, sweeping, fluid motion with no break in it. You need to have leverage on your opponent through strength, position, or both, for this to work. Even with the leverage, however, surprise is the key to gaining sufficient momentum to pull it off. If you hesitate or stop at any point; if you let the pressure off his blade for even a moment, he can disengage and escape.

3) There is a variation on disarm number 2 that is more delicate to achieve but requires the presence (or illusion) of quickness instead of strength. From a left flank parry with a lefthand weapon, rotate your wrist—a righthand weapon is already in position. Curl the blade very quickly from its inside blocking position under your opponent's blade, moving in a clockwise circle so that your blade comes under the opponent's blade and up the other

side. You now force his blade back through the center space between you and, after it has passed to the other side, curl your blade over on top of his and force it to the floor. Your blade has started on your left side, point down. It has described an arc of 270 degrees, curling under and then over your opponent's blade as it went through the arc, and never allowing contact to lapse.

To do the same thing from a right flank parry, you would first have to rotate your blade 360 degrees by turning arm, elbow, and wrist in the direction of your thumb. You start with the sharp edge of the blade in contact for the parry, and after the rotation of 360 degrees you have the sharp edge of your blade in contact again. Only now your hand, wrist, and arm are in position to make a strong whipping movement to your left. Before, in the original parrying position, they were in a weak position from which you could get no leverage.

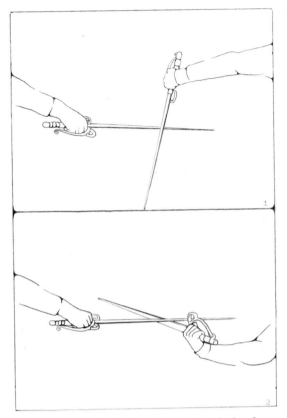

Figure 56 *Blade disarm: sword, right hand*

Figure 57 *Flight-path arc of a right flank cut*

You can do disarms, right or left, from shoulder parries just as you can from flank parries. It is simply a matter of finding the angle of the blade attack and the proper rotation of your hand and blade that will allow you to get your blade over and on top of your opponent's blade. If you start from your parry position and move in extreme slow motion you should be able to discover the proper angle and arc to achieve the disarm.

From a shoulder parry, when your blade is already pointing up on an inside position, you simply roll it over on top of the attacker's blade and force it down. That is simpler than a flank parry-disarm because the arc of the movement is shorter. You have less movement to achieve in disarms number 2 and 3, and about the same distance as in disarm number 1.

You can't really get leverage from a head parry to roll over on top of your opponent's blade, not unless you are 18 inches taller than he is, and so I don't recommend trying blade disarms from a head parry. If you must disarm from a head parry do it with "street tactics."

OFFENSIVE AND DEFENSIVE ARCS

For our purposes, the "arc" is defined as both the flight path and the distance that a weapon travels to either deliver or parry a blow.

The flight path of the weapon has to be kept clear. Let us say your assailant is facing stage right. If the assailant goes for a right shoulder cut on his opponent, with a 36-inch-long sword, his blade will describe an arc through the air upstage of him the diameter of which is the combined length of his arm and the sword. Therefore anything or anyone up to 6 feet upstage of him and more than waist high is in the path of that blade as he makes his cut. That is the flight path. When you choreograph a sword fight, you must take into account the presence of other actors, set pieces, furniture, drapes, and all set dressings. Be sure your combatants always have enough space around them to use their weapons without catching their blades on extraneous objects or people. This is especially dangerous, and therefore especially important, when you are choreographing a mass brawl or battle scene with many pairs or trios of combatants on stage at once. Actors in unrelated combats can strike each other inadvertently if flight paths are not carefully measured and cleared.

The other factor in arc is the distance a blow travels before it lands. The rule of thumb here is that the offensive arc must always exceed the defensive arc. In its simplest terms, if the defender is to have a proper margin of safety, the attacker's blade has to travel farther than the defender's blade before they meet. The absolute minimum is a ratio of 1:1 where both blades travel the same distance; and that is a bad ratio, one that invites accidents. Anything less, anything where the attacker's blade has a shorter route than the defender's blade, ought to result in a "hit." That's fine if you planned it that way, but if you want your combatant to parry a blow successfully, give him a chance to do so.

The minimum comfortable ratios are between 1.5:1 and 2:1. If you go from a right flank cut on the first beat of a fight to a left flank cut on the second beat, then the attacker has to arc his horizontal blade in a wide circular motion all the way over his head, an arc of perhaps 10 to 12 feet. The defender meanwhile simply moves his vertical blade from his left side to his right, keeping it point down. That is a distance of perhaps 3 feet. The ratio on this exchange of offensive to defensive arc is almost 4:1. That is a very safe ratio. It means that the attacker can whip his sword around as hard and as fast as he possibly can. With a 4:1 ratio he cannot get his blade there before the defender is ready for him. Most cuts and parries work well within the 1.5:1 to 2:1 ratio range. Thrusts are a little harder to arrange with adequate margin for safety on the part of the person parrying.

The purpose of setting this rule—that the offensive arc must always be longer than the defensive arc when a parry is to be successful —is to provide both margin for error and adequate reaction time for the defender. The defender may forget his next move for a fraction of a second; he remembers as he sees his opponent's blade start to move into the next agreed-upon blow. If a 2:1 ratio exists, the defender will still have enough reaction time to achieve his parry.

When both combatants are very well rehearsed and have never lost their place in the choreography, there still remains the problem of creating an illusion of reality and spontaneity. Just as it is distressing to hear an actor

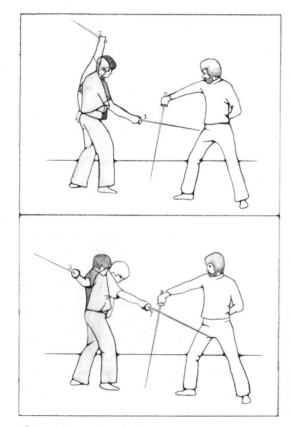

Figure 58 *Arc ratio of 4:1—safe choreography*

answer a question that has not been fully asked yet, or to watch him reach for a telephone that isn't going to ring for half a second, it is distressing for director and audience alike to see combatant "B" swing his blade into an overhead parry when combatant "A" hasn't yet started his move or in any way indicated that an overhead cut is on its way. In terms of sheer acting motivation, "B" can't start a parry until he sees "A" start an attack. That means "B" is always starting his move a fraction of a second behind "A." That's why he has to have the margin of the shorter arc to parry the blow successfully. A good 1.5:1 to 2:1 ratio makes sense for both aesthetics and safety.

RHYTHMICS AND STRUCTURE

The details and procedures of choreography will be discussed in a later chapter. At this juncture it is sufficient to point out that a combat is a story within the story of the play. It has a beginning, a middle, and an end. It has a rhythmic sense of its own. It has a structural sense of its own. Each combat is determined by the nature of the characters who are in conflict. Each is unique, and each should be exciting in its own way. Try to avoid metronomic predictability in the rhythm or frequency of blows: 1 . . . 2–3–4 . . . 5 . . . 6–7–8 is a lot more exciting than 1 . . . 2 . . . 3 . . . 4 . . . 5 . . . 6 . . . 7 . . . 8. By the same token the size, angle, target, and ferocity of the blows should vary throughout the fight. A steady déjà-vu pattern of "cut to head, cut to right flank, cut to left flank (yawn), thrust home under upstage arm," all of which could be accompanied by the measured 4/4 cadence of a Sousa Marching Band, will not generate the desired excitement. You want a sense of spontaneity and of inventiveness. Rhythmics and structure will help you achieve them.

CHOREOGRAPHY AND KINESTHETIC LEARNING

Obviously sword fights cannot be "freeform," and genuine "spontaneity" is what got

Laurence Olivier all those slash marks he speaks so fondly of. No, swordplay must be very carefully worked out and planned each step of the way. The fight is divided into beats.

1) The first logical step is to set the relative foot positions of the combatants. How far away from each other are they on any given beat? In what direction are they facing? Where are their feet and toes pointing? What guard are they in (attack, defense, or neutral)?

2) What foot action is involved in the beat? Do they stride in? Retreat? Right foot or left?

3) What arm motions are involved? If a sword is being swung, what is the flight path, the angle of attack and/or defense? Is the flight path clear of extraneous obstruction? What is the length of the arc? Is it long (or short) enough to be safe?

4) Do the offensive and defensive weapons meet at the proper angle and position?

5) Are both combatants comfortable and on balance in following through with this beat?

6) Does it *look* good?

7) Does it feel right for the characters in the situation?

When you have answered all these questions to your satisfaction through very slow-motion action and adjustment, you have choreographed one beat, or one exchange of blows. You are now ready to have the swords meet for a second time and to go through the same checklist again.

Start practicing your choreography in very slow motion until it is kinesthetically secure. Then increase it to half-speed and practice until kinesthetically secure, then up a notch at a time. You should not reach full-speed rehearsal for a long time. Don't rush this. Make sure your people are kinesthetically secure at each level of speed before they go to the next one. My own rule of thumb is that they must do the entire fight, without one error, five times at 50 percent of speed before they can increase it to 60 percent. If they make an error on the twenty-third beat of the fifth time through—too bad. Back they go to count one of the first time through, and four more to go. The same test must be passed to go from 60 percent tempo to 70 percent, and so on. My actors cannot even attempt the test to get out of the 50 percent of tempo limit until they have practiced the whole fight in slow motion thirty to forty times.

WARMUP AND PRACTICE

You should choreograph a sword fight at the same time, or on the same days, that you initially block that part of the play. Don't put it off. The combatants will be able to take advantage of every extra day of practice they are afforded to become both kinesthetically secure and visually polished.

Always warm up before starting to practice a fight. Do bends, stretches, and other calisthenics. You don't want to pull a muscle on stage. Warm up!

Once you have integrated the fight into the rehearsals, then if you have had a day or a weekend off, practice that fight several times before rehearsal begins. Don't wait until the fight arrives within the rehearsal and see if you remember it. Even when you are in daily rehearsal and/or performance, always practice the fight at least once before the runthrough begins to make sure the combatants still have it "in their muscles" and reflexes.

CONSISTENCY IN WEAPONS

Different weapons in the same category— two rapiers, two broadswords, two Greek short swords—will have different weights and balances. Grips will feel different. They just do not handle the same. Therefore, always try to use the same weapon.

The best of all possible worlds is when the actor has the actual performance weapons in his hands from the first choreographing rehearsal, but this is not always possible. He may have to work with a rehearsal substitute for a while until the actual performance weapon comes into his possession. When it comes, check over the choreography again, slowly, to see if any adjustments need to be made in balance, arc, velocity, angle, etc., to accommodate the idiosyncrasies of the new weapon.

Once you have the actual performance weapon and have made any necessary adjustments in the choreography, then set that weapon, mark it. Do not ever change or substitute weapons for the ones you have been rehearsing with. The actor has become used to the idiosyncrasies of his own weapon, and a new weapon may be enough to throw the choreography off and cause an accident.

MAINTAINING WEAPONS

Whether purchased from a professional armory house, rented from a costumer, or made in your own shop, swords require constant and careful maintenance. It is not so much that they will give you frequent trouble; if made well, they probably won't. The point is that checking them over daily can prevent an accident. There are four things to keep track of:

1) Keep blades and handles tightly and securely fitted. Don't let them wobble.

2) Keep the blades clean and rust-free. Oil and scour the blades whenever necessary to keep them looking well. Because swords pick up nicks and notches from being clashed together, there is always the possibility of someone's scratching himself just a bit on the blade. A clean, nonrusty blade is less likely to cause tetanus.

3) Always be sure the points of the swords are rounded off. A rounded tip that breaks off on the floor or in collision with another blade becomes a nasty jagged tip. Round it off again.

4) For the same reason, always check the edges and see that they remain blunted. They

may have been blunted last week when you got them, but six rehearsals have caused nicks and notches. They still are not sharp, but now they may have many ragged little indentations, each of them a tiny hook to catch a costume or scratch a finger. File the hooks down. Smooth the blades out. Keep those blades as safe as possible.

Summary

Above all, avoid the Errol Flynn syndrome and handle swords with respect. If you remember that they are tools of the stage and not toys, you have already gone a long way toward handling them safely and well.

Don't worry about achieving a "classic" swordsman's position. Until the 17th century there wasn't one to learn! Even after that it was still a matter of balance, and what was most comfortable for the individual. Find the stance, *approximating* the guard, that feels best to you. Don't try to copy the fencing master unless you are comfortable doing so. I envision Andrew Aguecheek from *Twelfth Night* at about 6'6" and 130 pounds. I envision the Earl of Douglas from *Henry IV, Part I* at 6'6" and 260 pounds. Can you imagine either one trying to copy the other's stance? I can't—not without a smile, anyway. Do your own thing!

For the actor, the rules and suggestions for cut, thrust, parry, and disarm are mostly common sense. Find the moves in your own body with your own balance. Learn to do them slowly and carefully, without rushing or being rushed, and you'll be fine. If your director and/or partner say "For heaven's sake, aren't you ready yet?" and you are not really secure, please say "No!" and stay at slow motion until you are secure. You will all be happier in the long run for your doing that, and possibly healthier, too.

Chapter IX

THE USE OF WEAPONS, SHIELDS, AND ARMOR IN STAGE COMBAT

SWORDS

The sword is an ancient and honorable weapon, though often used dishonorably and for dishonorable purposes. It has varied widely in shape and length during the centuries, but has always had a single purpose: to kill! The military strategist's notion of the best way to kill someone dictated the changes in sword design, as length, designed for reach, gave way to strength and weight for power. Copper gave way to brass, which gave way to iron, which gave way to steel. When the steel became strong enough so that a light blade could stop (parry) a heavier one, then the rapier developed and speed became preferable to weight and power.

Naturally, older styles of swords were not discarded when new ones were developed, and so fights often occurred between combatants with different types of weapons. Military maneuver also affected choice and design. Thus long, narrow-bladed swords were used by light infantry for skirmishing in both Greek and Roman armies. The Greek and Roman short sword was used by the heavy infantry, the phalanx, which maneuvered and wheeled en masse, always presenting a solid front of shields from which issued the short, wide-bladed stabbing sword that had great thrusting power. Individual maneuvering room to wield a long sword was not available in this shoulder-to-shoulder marching "tank," and so the short sword was better. We can therefore envision a combat between a "light" and a "heavy"

infantryman using different weapons and techniques.

In Elizabethan times, men of fashion started bringing rapier and dagger weapons and techniques home from the continent, while more conservative types still preferred the traditional broadsword and buckler. Thus we have historical record of duels between combatants using the two different types and sets of weapons.

The net effect is that there are many shapes, lengths, and types of sword, but they break down into three categories of usage that cross class lines, oceans, and centuries: 1) one-hand swords, used with a shield; 2) longer two-hand swords; and 3) one-hand swords used alone.

One-hand swords, used with a shield

These weapons include Greek, Roman, medieval, and Elizabethan weapons. The shields will be discussed in the next section, but their presence, in a wide variety of shapes and sizes, indicates that the swords were used almost entirely for offensive purposes unless the shield was lost. The weapons can be used for slashing, cutting, punching, or thrusting. These are almost all heavy-bladed weapons that lend themselves to full body participation (under isometric control) in the attacking stroke. They can be used to attack any part of the body.

The basic body relationship between combatants is square-on. This kind of sword and shield combat doesn't work too well from long distance. The combatants may circle each other outside of swords' reach for a while as they lunge and feint, trying to size each other up. When one or both make their move, however, they close in on each other, making use of the sword *hilt* available as a weapon, along with feet, knees, etc. Because the weapons are not particularly heavy or cumbersome, the combatants are relatively maneuverable and a great deal of footwork can be included in the fight. If you wish, your combatants can utilize a good portion of the stage in their give and take as they turn and wheel seeking advantage, trying to get past each other's shields.

Fights with these types of weapons, particularly including the rapier and dagger (which served the function of a shield and could also be turned to offensive use), give you great flexibility in choice of tempo, in gross maneuverability of the combatants across and around the stage, and in the flexibility of weapon maneuverability for an interesting variety of blow and parry.

Long two-hand swords

The full-fledged two-hand broadsword doesn't appear until the 15th century and is gone by the end of the 16th century. However, somewhat shorter and lighter hand-and-a-half broadswords have a somewhat longer life span. This type of weapon coincided with the introduction of plate armor in the 14th century and was designed to compensate for and smash through the added protection the armor gave its wearer.

The two-hand broadsword reached a length of 6 feet and was not used by the knight in armor. It was a foot soldier's weapon for use against his counterpart, and a pole-type defensive weapon to keep the armor-plated horseman away from him. As we are unlikely to have horses on stage, most two-hand broadsword combats will be between two unarmored infantrymen. If a knight or any other combatant handles the "sword of war" (one-and-a-half-hand broadsword) with two hands, then the basic techniques employed become the same as for the two-hand broadsword. The broadsword was used for both offense and defense.

Although the tip is sharp and may be used for thrusting, and the handle is heavy and may be used for punching, the primary use of a two-hand broadsword is for cutting and/or impact effect. The blade is very heavy, and the full weight of the body is required to swing it with authority. Almost all blows are wide, sweeping cuts. The blades are often kept in continuous motion, in a series of figure 8's effected by rotating the wrists at the end of each arc and pulling the blade back over the other way.

Cuts and parries follow the same rules as for other swords: they should aim at the target, meet in the middle of the blades, meet with the sharp or forehand edges, and meet at 90 degrees if possible. Because of the weight and achieved velocity of the attacking blade at the point of impact, the parry cannot be made by placing and holding the defensive blade in the correct position. The defensive blade would be driven right back into the defender by the force of the blow received. The defender must swing his blade into the parry position at full strength to meet the attacking blade. Even with isometric control on the part of the combatants to reduce the impact, and to even it out in case of a wide disparity in weight or strength between the two, the impact is going to be considerable. You will need strong hands and wrists to handle a two-hand broadsword fight.

Be aware of the need to "even out" a competition between two men of differing size and strength by the degree of isometric restraint each one employs. Many years ago, at age 22 and in reasonably good condition at 200 pounds, I engaged in broadsword play with an actor who was in excellent shape at 260 pounds. I had choreographed the fight and coached the actor in question, who was really trying not to knock me clear into the sixth row of the mezzanine. We were doing *Henry IV, Part I,* and I was playing King Henry. I was not supposed to win the fight with this massive Earl of Douglas, but I was supposed to hold out long enough for my son, Prince Hal, to come to my rescue. It was a near thing each night, and my arms ached—260 pounds of football player matched against 200 pounds of football watcher was a bit much, even with his help and restraint. In a real fight I would have been beaten into the ground on the first or second exchange.

Also be aware that the length of the blades makes a "mid-blade meet" somewhat difficult to achieve from a fully upright position. In order to achieve a left flank parry, you need to take a virtual baseball-bat swing, including

Figure 59 *Overhead parry with a two-hand broadsword*

"the stride into the pitch," to bring your blade into position with sufficient velocity to neutralize the attack. This means striding with your left foot and swinging your fulcrum of balance in the hips to the left to support the arm movement.

The most difficult parry with broadsword is the overhead parry. Your opponent is still trying to split you down the middle, so his blade is coming down in a line with the bridge of your nose. In order to get the middle of your blade at the point of impact, you are going to have 3 feet of steel plus the handle coming off to the right or left of that point. Unless you have an extraordinary build, this means that, if you are standing straight up, your hands are 2 feet outside of one of your shoulders. Well, you can't get any strength or support that way! You have to plant one foot and slide the other foot out in the direction of the sword handle, so that you get your trunk and spine underneath your hands to help absorb the shock of impact. If you are right-handed you will get more support strength if you slide toward your left. So, as your opponent starts his cut:

a) Extend both arms fully and get your sword over your head, parallel to the ground.

b) Plant your right foot where it is, but cheat the width of your stance so that your feet start from a base of 14 to 18 inches instead of shoulder width apart.

c) Slide your left foot out roughly 2 feet so that it is planted about 3½ feet from your right foot and about a foot farther out than your head, which is now lined up underneath your hands.

d) Lock your right knee and push off.

e) Flex your left knee and bend it a bit to give you solidity in this extrawide stance, with balance, as the attacking blade comes down on the middle of your sword, at a point some 18 inches above where your head was before you started your defensive maneuver.

f) You are slightly off balance to your left

now; but with your left knee bent, you are already in position to thrust off of your left foot and come back onto your guard the moment you have absorbed the impact of the blow and disengaged.

Thrusts, punches, and trips can be executed fairly quickly in a broadsword fight, and because of this they can provide variety of tempo and rhythm, as well as variety of attack plan. Cuts, however, are another story. The weight and length of the blades make the cutting motions slow, heavy, and ponderous. The blades are hard to maneuver. Actors cannot dart around and swing their swords at the same time. You have to plant your feet to attack. The defender can either move his feet and evade the attack, or he can plant his own feet and parry. Neither combatant can realistically run and swing at the same time. This means that a broadsword fight is relatively stable (if you are an optimist) or static (if you are a pessimist). It cannot have the same degree of grace, agility, or mobility to be found in combat with sword and buckler or in one-hand sword fights. The whole rhythm of the fight will be slower and heavier than fights with lighter weapons. If you start planning your fight with this in mind, you can either accentuate it to create a feeling of sweaty, animalistic menace; or you can plan relatively few cuts and throw in a lot of thrusts, feints, punches, and footwork.

One-hand swords, used alone

Rapiers, and then the short sword, come into vogue in the late 16th century. Gradually, the use of shield or dagger (in effect, the use of the left hand) for defense, disappears. The basic body position becomes side to side. Foot positions for neutral guard, attack, and retreat were noted earlier, in Chapter VIII. In one-hand swordplay, the sword is used for both offense and defense. The weapons are designed for cutting, thrusting, and punching (although thrusting becomes more and more

prominent) until we reach the foil, which has a round blade and can be used only for thrusting. Attack and defense maneuvers with these weapons are also noted in Chapter VIII.

As the left hand is free, it does have some possibilities. Primarily it is carried curled behind the head, for balance. If it is gloved, it can be used to try to rip the sword out of the opponent's grasp. It can also grab for a makeshift shield, a cloak, dirt to throw in an opponent's eyes, etc., but this comes under the heading of "battlefield techniques" and is not part of the swordplay itself.

The blades on all of these weapons are light, flexible, and very quick. They can be easily maneuvered with the fingers and wrist, as well as with the whole arm. In fact you will want to employ wider arcs in your offensive and defensive blows than is realistically proper, and employ more body support than is realistically necessary—both for dramatic effect.

The combatants wear no heavy armor, and the weapons are extensions of the combatants' arms. They do not encumber them or hamper them in any way. You can therefore employ any combination or variation of blocking, footwork, gymnastics, rhythms, tempos, and/or other theatrics you wish. You are limited by the requirements of safety and by your imagination, not by the nature or physical properties of the weapons.

SHIELDS AND ARMOR

The variety of shields and armor available to you for stage use will be much smaller and more limited than the variety depicted and described in the books and art works of libraries and museums. If you are renting or borrowing armor you will be able to get pieces that are in or near the period you want, but each period had variety and overlap in it, and the complete range will not be available. When the costumes arrive, your armor and shields will be reproductions of the original pieces, not antiques. They will most likely be made of celastic or some similar fiberglass or plastic material. They will *look* fine, if the costume house takes pride in its reputation, but they will not be the real thing. This is both an asset and a liability.

It is an asset because a full suit of the real thing weighed almost 200 pounds (for both rider and steed) in 1450, and helmets alone weighed between 13 and 24 pounds.[1] Real armor was terribly heavy, hot, and hard to move in. The replicas available to you, in modern materials, are featherweight by comparison and much more comfortable. "Chain mail" is often knitted from metallicized yarn!

The liability is that you cannot use the armor as though it were real because it is not. You want to maintain the illusion of mass and of metal, and to do this you must avoid creating the dull, flat sound of metal on fiberglass. So you do not plan to strike the armor with a metal weapon.

It is not my purpose in this book to describe or depict the historically accurate armor of any period. I can only point out that this information is available in books and art works. When you have determined the location and period in which you wish to set your production, you can research the appropriate armor and then decide how much of it you wish to use and how you are going to acquire it. Once you have it, come back to this chapter, and we'll talk about how to use it.

If you have the resources of money, space, and personnel to buy the materials and build your own, then, with diligent research into art works and books, you can determine the exact type, nature, composition, and style of armor you want. You can then re-create it for yourself and have the exact piece or pieces that you desire. Once again, however, you will have replicas made to look like ancient pieces, but made in reality from modern lightweight materials. They will not stand up to a battering with steel weapons, and the "clang" of a

steel weapon on your helmet or breast-plate will sound terribly wrong.

Shields are another matter. You can obtain or construct wooden or metal shields that can be wielded with great effect. Again, the degree of historical accuracy is a matter of taste, research, and tenacity. Each era had a variety of shields in use. Within each era and location, they varied in size, shape, and decoration. During the 5th century the Greeks used, for example, a crescent-shaped shield and a round shield about 18 inches in diameter for light infantry, and a very large round shield of 2½ to 3 feet in diameter for the heavy "hoplite" infantry. In earlier periods the Greek shield was between 3 and 5 feet in length and shaped like a figure 8, with a width of perhaps 14 inches at the waist. Other hoplite shields were oval, not round. They were about 4 feet long and perhaps 18 to 24 inches wide.

These are just the Greek shields. The Romans used a variety of round and oval shields until they settled on a heavy rectangular shield for their phalanx. In the Dark Ages and medieval times, depending on the tribe or nationality involved, shields might be of wood, wood-rimmed and reinforced with metal, or metal. They might be "targets" or "bucklers" of small diameter; they might be "kite shields," which were triangular in shape and up to 6 feet in height. They might be round, oval, square, rectangular, triangular, and I am sure that someone, somewhere, built one in the shape of a trapezoid, even if he didn't know the name for it. There are too many possibilities to be enumerated here. As with the other armor pieces, it is a matter for the director and/or designer to work out by doing their research and then choosing the appropriate design for their character in his milieu. I am not concerned here with your choice, but rather with how you use the shield you have.

Use for defense

For the actor and choreographer, using the shield for defense is a matter of common sense

---

[1] Ffoulkes, Charles. *The Armourer and His Craft.* New York: Benjamin Blom, 1967, p. 119.

and individual ability. Primarily, you keep it between the attacking blade and your body or head. Try to take the attacking blow at or near the center of the shield to give yourself the maximum margin for error. Try to have the face of the shield meet the blade at a 90-degree angle.

The size and weight of the actor relative to the size and weight of the shield will determine the way in which it is handled, as much as or more than will the original intent of the shield's designer. The way a shield was handled on its contemporary battlefield by the individual soldier was usually "the best I can" as opposed to "regulation fashion." There are exceptions to this, of course. The correct angle and height at which the shield was held to form a wall for the Greek hoplite and the Roman phalanx was very important and was strictly adhered to. You are unlikely to use a phalanx too often on stage, however. Most of your sword and shield combats will be individual, and thus individual size, strength, and idiosyncrasy will come into play. Given the same shield—let us say an oval shield 4 feet long and 2 feet wide at its widest point, made of metal and grasped with heavy leather arm-loop and hand grip—a 260-pound actor will handle it with his forearm. He will hold it away from his body, maneuvering it lightly and quickly. He will be able to do things with it that a 160-pound actor will find impossible. For example the 260-pound man can use this shield to sweep aside an oncoming blade; he is strong enough to move the shield out to meet the attacking cut. The 160-pound actor is more likely to use the shield more conventionally. He will get his elbow tight into his side and pull the shield in close to his body. He will move it to the best position to ward off a blow, but he won't swing it. He can't. He uses it to accept and absorb a blow, not for counterforce that might help neutralize the power of an attacking blow.

Essentially there are two types of shields, regardless of their shape or their time and place of origin: arm shields and body shields. An arm shield is a small shield that can be maneuvered by the arm of the defender alone and is used to "pick off" or deflect a blow as frequently as it is to block or absorb one. Such a shield is light and maneuverable. In rapier and dagger fights, the dagger serves the same function. The main characteristic of this type of shield is its maneuverability. It can be shifted about quickly and swung into defensive position quickly. Thus, the defender does not have to hold his left arm in front of himself continually and can therefore use that arm for balance and other maneuvers. He can whip the shield back into a defensive guard quickly enough if he is threatened.

The body shield is the large shield that serves as a defensive wall to cover most or all of the body. It may be round like the Greek hoplite's, rectangular like the Roman legionary's, triangular like the kite shield of the medieval knight, or it may be oval. In any case it is large, heavy, and relatively immobile. And you do not move it around too much! It is held close in to the body with the arm locked into the body for support. It protects its wearer from a missile or a blow by being impenetrable and massive. It may remain relatively static instead of moving out to meet a blow, but it is massive and solid and can shake off the missile or blow without being driven back into the bearer, who throws his weight into support of the shield and shield arm. That, of course, presumes relative equality of size and strength between attacker and defender. If they are widely disparate, then all bets are off. The key to handling the body shield is that you take refuge behind it, whereas you maneuver the arm shield. You are relying more on power and stamina in the weaponry that includes the body shield, and more on quickness, dexterity, and maneuverability in the weaponry that includes the arm shield.

The medieval kite-shield, at 6 feet in height, is always a body shield, no matter who is handling it. The dagger that goes with a rapier, and the target, are always arm shields, no matter who is handling them. There are a number of shields that fall in the middle. They are a little too big always to handle gracefully or a little too small for a big man to shelter behind, and sometimes they are both at once! A Mycenaean Greek shield 3½ feet long and 18 inches at the waist of a figure 8 design might present such a problem. It might be a bad choice by the costumer for any specific actor. But if the actor and costumer have no choice, make do! There is no right way to handle that shield for defensive purposes. The actor who has been given it will have to work it out as best he can, with his director and according to his particular physical gifts.

The armor that you will wear on stage can serve only a cosmetic costume function. It is not constructed to accept the kind of punishment and afford the kind of protection of its historical counterpart. Your shield and sword may be of steel, but your helmet is of tin at best, and probably of some form of plastic. Your breastplate, backplate, and arm and leg pieces all are of plastic or fiberglass. If you are wearing "chain mail," it is made of knitted yarn! Your "leather" may be pressed board. In other words you are not wearing armor, whatever the mirror may tell you. One good hard whack with a sword, mace, or battle-ax will certainly shatter the illusion for the audience and may shatter the actor as well. Other than providing motivation for the actor to be tired and encumbered by "all that steel," the sum total of realistic defensive use to which you can put your armor is: *ZERO!* Just let it hang there and look good. Rely on your sword and shield for all defensive combat effects and maneuvers.

Use for offense

In discussing the use of armor for offense in stage combat, you are dealing with a great deal more than cosmetics. Just how inventively and effectively you can use it depends in large measure on what pieces you are wearing.

A helmet with a rounded top and brim is of little use offensively for butting, whereas a helmet with a spike on the crest is very good for it. You can't actually jam your head into the body or throat or face of your opponent without causing injury, but you can create that illusion by jamming your head into the target off to one side. The right hemisphere of your helmet, for example, is thrust into the right pectoral area of your opponent, with the spike passing (like a sword thrust) between his side and his right arm, under the armpit. It is an unexpected move and can be quite effective. If the right hemisphere of your helmet jams into the right-side neck muscles of your opponent and the spike passes upstage of his neck, the effect can be even more spectacular. If the angle is properly set up, it will look as though you went straight into his throat.

Of course, you can remove the helmet and use it in your hand as an impact weapon. In addition, a wide-brimmed "wash-basin" type of helmet can be used as a cutting weapon if you take it in your hand and slash with the brim.

Shoulder pieces increase the visual impact of tackling. You can also get a good effect by setting your feet and swinging your torso to ram your shoulder into an opponent. If you are armored and he is not, you're hitting him with a steel impact weapon. If there is a sharp rim, or edge, or spike on the shoulder piece, you can use this "shoulder slap" for a cutting or stabbing attack.

Breast- and backplates are of little use as offensive weapons. First of all, they are hard to maneuver. Second, they rarely have any sharp protrusion or other factor of offensive capability. Again, if you are armored and your opponent is not, your armor gives you the added strength and crushing power of an artificial exoskeleton. If you are considerably larger than your opponent, you could wrap your arms around him and crush him to death in a "steel embrace." If your armor is embossed, or has a sufficient spike or protrusion on the breastplate, the embrace would "impale" your opponent (of course, you would have to pull him to you so that the spike passed upstage of his body).

Elbow pieces are fine offensive weapons, with or without spikes. Coming off a head cut or a head parry, either the attacker or defender can rotate his body, and particularly his right shoulder, upward toward his left, push off with his right foot, and while maintaining pressure on the opponent's blade, whip his elbow underneath the locked blades and up into the neck or jaw of his opponent. All parry positions carry with them "inside position." That means that the conclusion of almost any parry that leaves the defender erect and on balance also leaves the defender in good position to drive his elbow in a straight line into the torso or in a curving arc "into" (really past) the throat or head of his opponent. If the elbow armor piece is smooth, you have delivered an impact blow that should at least faze him, if not disable him. If the piece is spiked, the blow can be lethal. In the course of my career as a stage-fight director I have found the elbow piece to be a marvelous weapon and have used it for offense more than any other piece of armor. The stroke is short and quick. Both the visual and physical impact are great. It can come at almost any time from any angle, and it can be delivered to almost any target from the crotch to the face.

The use of the knees and feet are the same in armor as they are in street clothes. The difference lies only in the force of the blow delivered because of the "iron sheathing," which increases the impact.

The glove or gauntlet is also a potential offensive weapon. A backhand slap delivered with a gauntlet has terrific force to it, and if brought across the face can "blind" an opponent.

In handling your armor as an offensive weapon, be aware of the dangers involved. If you are working with slashes or cuts or thrusts from various sharpened portions of your armor follow the safety rules and procedures laid down in Chapter VII on "The Use of Weapons." Where you are using smooth or blunt portions of your armor for impact weapons, follow the safety rules and procedures laid down in Chapters III and IV on "Body Blows" and "Head Blows." The backhand slap with a gauntlet is a head blow that must *not* land. Use the "go-by" procedure for a head punch, described in Chapter IV, not the slapping technique of Chapter III. If you slap someone with the back of a fiberglass gauntlet, never mind a metal one, you will well nigh tear his head off. The fact that armor is heavy would make it motivationally proper to move in larger and slower arcs than you would use fighting in conventional clothes. This gives you an added margin of safety in the planning and execution of these exchanges.

Arm shields can be used offensively far more easily than body shields, simply because they are lighter and more maneuverable. An arm shield is small enough and light enough to be flipped horizontally, while still being properly held by the arm-loop and grip, and smashed into an opponent rim first. If you bring the edge down on his shoulder, you will disable that arm. A blow with the rim into an unprotected side or abdomen should double him over. If you bring it down on his neck, you can kill him. Holding the shield vertically in normal defensive position doesn't prevent you from attacking with it, using it as a battering ram; and if it has a spike, it is a thrusting weapon as well. The dagger used with a rapier as an "arm shield" has such obvious offensive capabilities that they need not be described here.

A body shield is harder to use offensively, but it is by no means impossible. If your character has lost his offensive weapon, then he can use his right hand to maneuver the pitch of the shield and bring the rim to bear as a weapon. Adding the right hand to the left gives you plenty of power to swing the heavy shield as an impact weapon. If the shield is rectangular, or if it is a triangular kite shield, it has some sharp points on its perimeter. These can be used to thrust.

In one fight I choreographed, one character killed another by thrusting the sharp bottom point of his kite shield into a fallen opponent like a spear, after both had lost their offensive weapons. In another production a few years later, the hero lost his sword and was left with only his kite shield for defense. The villain crowed in triumph and charged at him almost the full width of the stage with his sword held high and his own shield, seemingly unneeded, off to one side. At the last moment the hero, who had been down on one knee holding his shield over his body in a conventional defensive guard, slid the shield off his arm, flipped it horizontal to the floor, braced the top of it with both hands and his chest, and the villain impaled himself on the pointed bottom of it.

That's pretty hard to do with a round Greek hoplite shield, but you can effect a gash with the corner of a Roman legionary rectangular shield or any corner of a triangular shield. You can also use the broad heavy face of a body shield for a ram. The weight and size of it can pin an opponent against a wall, a tree, a set piece, or the floor. If there is enough weight and power behind the move, the shield can be a lethal crushing weapon. If there is a spike on it, it becomes a stabbing or thrusting weapon as well. On a heavy shield, this would be more like the terrifyingly inexorable action of the "iron maiden" than like the quick thrust of a sword.

Like everything else we have described, these moves are not without risk. With shields, as with armor, refer to the appropriate sections of Chapters III, IV, and VII for safety rules and procedures before incorporating these moves into your choreography. In Chapter VII I noted the difference between "gen-tleman's rules" and "battlefield conditions." In a contest situation, a trial of skill with rules and a judge or referee to enforce them, and where life is not at stake, gentleman's rules can and usually do prevail. Under those conditions virtually none of the offensive techniques for the use of shield or armor that I have outlined in this chapter would come into play. Shields and armor are defensive only, in intent, and it would not be proper to use them in any other way. That would be considered trickery and "beneath a gentleman." These techniques apply quite cheerfully and regularly to the battlefield, the courtyard, and the alley, where life is held more dear than "honor," and the substance of walking away from the fight under your own power is held in more esteem than "doing it right."

Earlier I noted that you want to achieve spontaneity and freshness in your choreography, so that the audience is caught by surprise. The use of shield and armor as offensive weapons affords fine opportunities for you to achieve this goal.

SPEARS AND POLEARMS

The first blunt instrument used by one humanoid against another may well have been a rock. As mayhem preceded literacy we cannot be sure of this point. If the rock was first, then the fallen branch or other piece of stout wood was surely next. The advantage of a long weapon over a shorter one soon became apparent, as did the advantage of tapering and sharpening the weapon so that it would penetrate the opponent's body. These wooden weapons soon diverged into two classifications. On the one hand we developed long, narrow weapons that were quick to handle and highly maneuverable for purposes of slashing, cutting, tripping, stabbing, and other dexterous infliction of injury. These became the quarterstaff, spear, and halberd. The other group of weapons stayed relatively short in length, but developed mass and crushing power. Among these are the club, battle-ax, hammer, and mace. In this section we shall deal with spears and polearms; in the next with crushing or impact weapons.

Man is a variable creature, hard to predict in many ways. In one thing he is consistent. From the first irritated man-ape clouting his neighbor with a dead branch to a contemporary Neanderthal laying out his erstwhile pool partner with the butt of a cue, man has had a fondness for polearms. They are remarkably flexible in the ways they can be used. They vary in length, thickness, and the hardware on the business end according to the era and geographical location of your characters, but the entire historical range of polearms is not available to you for a series of simple and pragmatic reasons.

A short throwing spear, such as the Greek javelin or the African assegai, is not used in stage combat for throwing purposes. A character may carry it and fight with it, but only as a thrusting weapon, usually in conjunction with a shield. There is no safe way to throw a spear, or knife, at someone on stage if it is intended to hit the target. There is no safe way to fake it. A spear thrown hard enough to travel 10 feet in a straight line is moving at a lethal rate of speed. You may be able to imagine an actor willing to trust his partner's accuracy and able to catch the spear shaft under his upstage arm. I *cannot* imagine it. I would never plan it. I would never allow it. You can have a spear thrown on stage that is intended to travel far upstage of the "target" character and land in a well-prepared and very large reinforced target. It can go offstage and strike a target set up in the wings, or it can stick into a specially prepared wall of the stage set. This is stage action. It is not stage combat. The person throwing the spear is in reality relating to an immobile wooden target. The "intended victim" of the weapon is nothing more than motivation for an action that does not otherwise require his presence. Throwing a weapon like a spear, a knife, or an ax has a very excit-

ing potential on stage. The "thud" of the weapon into the receiving area and the sight of it quivering in the wall is very effective. If you have a balanced weapon, and an actor who can throw it well, use the business. It looks great. But never play the game of "I can duck out of the way." Never aim the weapon at an actor on the theory that he can duck in plenty of time because he knows it is coming. An actor can freeze, slip, forget, or just be slow. He needs to be wrong only once. If the flight path of the weapon is parallel to the audience, they will never see the margin of safety you have built into the flight path.

Do be sure that the flight path is parallel to, or away from, the audience and clear of everyone. The danger inherent in flinging weapons about is an obvious one, and ever present. It is one that must constantly be kept in mind. In July 1974 I attended a performance of *King Lear* at the Guthrie Theatre in Minneapolis. Michael Langham had either inserted or allowed a colorful piece of business in which one of Lear's retainers threw a spear at one of Goneril's retainers—"just to frighten him." The spear was thrown in fun and was obviously not meant to touch the servant in Goneril's household. It didn't. Instead it flew out into the house and landed point first in a front-row seat. The seat was empty at the time—good fortune for everyone involved.

At the other extreme, the hoplite spear, carried by the rear ranks of the advancing Greek armies, ranged from 16 to 21 feet in length. On a large number of stages in the United States, that spear point would be at, or past, stage center before the actor carrying the spear appeared from the wings. The weapon may be historically accurate, but it is too long, too unwieldy, for stage use.

The quarterstaff was roughly 6 feet long and about 1½ inches in diameter. Spears from all ages that you will use on stage tend to range from 5 to 7 feet in pole length and have an assortment of blade shapes adding another 12 to

18 inches. This general length of feet by 1½ inches in diameter is a nice workable weapon, and there are a number of things you can do with it.

If you are dealing with a quarterstaff that has no pointed end on it for stabbing, you cannot "penetrate" the body with it, but a quarterstaff or a pool cue can leave a mighty big bruise and cause some internal damage if the narrow end of it is jabbed into the abdomen. If jammed into the eye, it can blind. If jammed into the throat, it can kill. You can therefore use the quarterstaff and similar tubular but unpointed weapons to stab, in the same way you use a spear. The result of a successful "hit" will be different, and less than a hit with a pointed polearm, but the *action* is the same.

Pole weapons that have been equipped with a sharp tip include spears, halberds, pikes, etc. The variation is in the width and weight of the point or blade affixed to the end of the pole (or shaft). In almost all cases the handling is the same.

The tactics of pole weapons include cuts, thrusts, trips, and slashes. For each of these moves the weapon can be gripped at the end with both hands; with one hand at the butt and the other advanced 2 to 3 feet to the middle of the shaft; or with the hands 18 to 24 inches apart toward the center of the shaft. How you hold it depends on its weight and balance, your hand and wrist strength, and the action you are trying to accomplish. You can hold the spear toward the center of the shaft with your right hand, tuck the butt under your right arm, and use it with a shield. This reduces the maneuverability of the weapon, however, limiting you largely to thrusting actions.

When holding the polearm at the end in both hands and taking sweeping cuts at your opponent, you are both in the mode of the two-hand broadsword fight described earlier. The procedures for cut and parry for broadsword will apply except for the overhead parry (see p. 125). When you are thrusting with the

sharp end of the weapon, you are in the same mode as when thrusting with long swords, and the same procedures for attack and defense with thrusts, listed earlier in the chapter, apply. This is also true if you are fighting with spear and shield. You can turn aside a thrust with the shield with a beat parry, by setting up a "gate" with your own weapon, or by sidestep evasion.

You can do some things with polearms, however, that you cannot do with swords, if you are using them as your sole two-hand weapon, and these techniques are among the most fun. You have to hold a sword by the handle. The blade is theoretically sharp, and you would cut your hand if you grasped it in the middle. A polearm has a smooth shaft running for roughly 6 feet before you reach sharp metal, and a quarterstaff has no sharp metal at all. This means you can assume a square-on guard grasping a quarterstaff or spear in the middle of the shaft, with your hands spread 18 to 24 inches, hold it at arm's length in front of you parallel to the ground, and use either end for attack or defense. If your hands are spread 18 to 24 inches, there

Figure 60 *Square-on polearm grip (depicting a shoulder cut and parry)*

Figure 61 *Polearm overhead parry*

are 2 or more feet of shaft on the outside of each hand, which gives you enough margin for cut and parry on a very quick scale. You can attack with alternate blows to the opponent's side, head, shoulder, flank, and calf in succession with great speed. The cut and parry procedure is the same as with sword blades. Try to meet in the center of your 2- to 3-foot span outside your hand, and try to meet at right angles. For backhand overhead cuts, you can slide the left hand down to meet the right in a baseball grip; for forehand overhead cuts, you can slide the right hand down to meet the left. For an overhead parry slide both hands outward on the shaft about one foot to allow a safe 3- to 4-foot expanse in the center of your shaft for your opponent's shaft to land on without cracking your knuckles.

Trips can be attempted with one hand or two. From a two-hand center grip, you simply let go with one hand and sweep the blade across the opponent's ankles or shins from either side, pulling the shaft through its arc with the other hand. The opponent steps or jumps over the sweep, depending on whether it is choreographed to land or not. If the sweep is programmed to succeed, then he steps over the weapon and goes into a side-fall as his foot touches the ground again. If his leap is a successful evasion, he leaps and lands on both feet and is ready to continue the battle.

You can step to one side of your opponent, getting a little outside him to left or right, and sweep your shaft into the back of his ankles. You can go the other way and sweep it across the front of his shins. In either case the opponent follows the same procedure. He leaps over the shaft and then either continues the fight or goes into a front- or back-fall, depending on the direction of the offensive sweep and on the choreographer's intent.

You can turn your polearm toward your opponent, in a thrusting position, slide it low between his legs, and twist it sideways, so that the forward end of your shaft hooks the heel of one foot and the middle of the shaft hooks the shin of the other foot. That will spill him

Figure 62 *Polearm trip, between legs*

backward into a sit-down back-fall unless he evades the attack by leaping back from it or up over it.

Each of the above tripping maneuvers can also be achieved two-hand, if you have both hands down at the end of your weapon.

In each of these trips, of course, you are not actually taking your opponent off his feet. He leaps to avoid your shaft in all cases. If the script says he was too late, then it looks as if he was knocked off his feet. If his evasion was planned to be in time, then he looks as if he is clear. In reality, the actor must get clear of the pole. It is moving too fast for him to allow it to hit him and simply give way in front of it. He will be knocked off balance. The only exception is the last trip described, in which you are twisting the pole between his legs. There you are taking him down with leverage, not sweeping his legs out from under him. Thus, it is safe for him to let the pole reach his legs and then lead the pole as he takes himself into the sit-down back-fall.

All these moves are possible with a quarter-staff, walking stick, pool cue, or spear. The halberd and pike are spears with ax-blades and spikes on the end of them as well as a pointed tip. This makes them good slashing weapons, as well, from a two-hand guard. It also makes them good impact weapons when grasped at the end of the shaft and swung in a wide arc with both hands. This extra advantage is off-set by the fact that the added metal on the ax or spike end unbalances the weapon and makes it much more awkward to use from the center-grip position. If it is a heavier weapon than the spear or quarterstaff, it is also a slower one.

Polearms can provide some of the flashiest and most gymnastic scenes of fight choreography. Just don't get carried away, particularly when setting up the rapid-fire exchanges. The faster the action in the final production, the shorter the arcs for the offensive and defensive actors, the more slowly and carefully you must begin the process of setting up the

sequence, and the more slowly you must build up, notch by notch, to full speed.

CRUSHING—IMPACT WEAPONS

Crushing and impact weapons start with our Neanderthal tree branch and develop into a deliberately fashioned club, as a man chooses this weapon in preference to a sharpened or pointed spear. As technology improves and new materials become available, we have stone axes, then metal axes and clubs of copper, bronze, iron, and steel. Eventually we reach the Middle Ages, during which crushing weapons reach their height as an art form. Here we have the battle-ax, the hammer, the mace, and the flail.

The battle-ax is a cutting weapon, but its use depends entirely on power and force. It does not dart through a defense; it smashes through it. It was developed to cut through armor, and it will. An ax-head fitted to a spear shaft would be called a halberd, a poleax, or a "bill." With its butt set into the ground and supported, its length would do a decent defensive job of holding off an attacking horseman; and one could take a healthy swipe at him with the ax blade, swinging from the end of the shaft, as he rode by. Essentially, though, these are polearms and are treated in the previous section.

We are here concerned with a shorter-handled ax, perhaps 3 to 4 feet in length, which can be managed with one hand, leaving the left hand free to use a shield for defense, or with both hands. This ax is of little use for defense. It is purely offensive in nature and intent.

If wielded with one hand, the blow is weaker and can probably be stopped or at least deflected with a shield. If wielded with two hands, the force of the blow is well-nigh irresistible. The only fully effective defense against the ax blade is evasion. Even deflection of a two-hand ax blow takes its toll of the victim. The impact is enormous, and unless the angle of the ax blade is quite oblique, it will not glance off; it will cut through. You cannot parry an ax blow with a shield. However, you can successfully parry an attacking ax blow if you are using a broadsword or a polearm of your own and you parry the ax handle. In that case the force of the blade doesn't come fully into play. A meeting of an ax handle below the blade but still in the middle of the weapon, and a broadsword blade or polearm shaft can be a stalemate. This cannot realistically be achieved with a shield because its surface is too large. The ax blade is going to hit the shield surface somewhere and cleave right through it. If you do get the whole shield under the ax blade and try to hit the ax handle with it, then the centrifugal force of the swinging ax blade will carry it over and into the shoulder and/or torso that the shield is no longer protecting. When choreographing for battle-ax and shield, your options are limited.

You can have a "hit" and be done with it in one or two blows; or you can use evasion so that blows are ducked under, leaped over, or sidestepped; or you can try for a disarm. You cannot realistically have them hack away at each other for any length of time. The first "hack" that landed would disable; the second would kill. A man with a strong polearm or broadsword can keep inside the arc of the swinging ax and continually parry on the ax handle, but if he has a shield, he had better not try to use it.

An ax disarm can be done, but it is tricky. The ax blade usually is wider at its cutting edge than where it joins the handle. It will therefore have reverse curves in it. If the two ax handles meet underneath the blades and then slide down to lock blades at the inside curve of the metal, then a "tug of war" can ensue and one of the axes can be pulled free. This can be modified to have, for example,

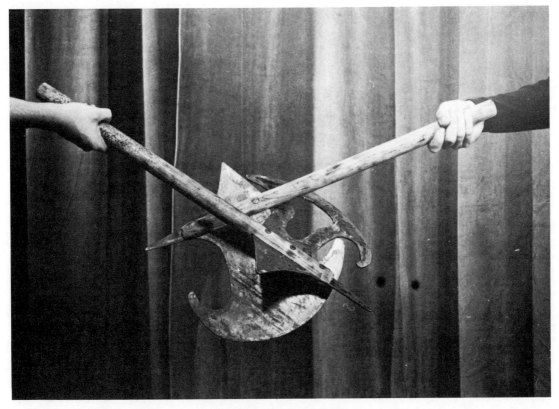

Figure 63 *Battle-ax disarm*

Macbeth and Macduff lock ax handles—Macbeth tries to disengage for another swing but Macduff quickly slides his ax down the remaining length of Macbeth's ax handle, locks blades, and yanks! If Macbeth is not ready for the move, he has lost his weapon. The halberd, poleax, pike, and bill have an inside curve on their blades and have a spike on their blades. In each case, then, a hooking implement exists on the weapon that makes it usable for a disarm by engaging the opponent's weapon in a standard parry and then sliding the "hook" into place and pulling the enemy's weapon out of his grasp.

The hammer, mace, and flail have no cutting edge. They rely on sheer crushing power, but that is considerable. Because they will not cut through a shield, they can be parried successfully with one. However, the blow would have to take some toll on the defender. The hammer is the heaviest of these weapons. It was about 4 feet in length and was in the shape its name suggests, with a spike often attached to the other side of the warhead. Swung with one hand, it was about as effective as the mace and flail, but it allowed its user to have a shield of his own for defense. Swung with two hands it was very powerful, but the wielder had no defense of his own. The warrior with a mace or a flail usually carried a shield as well.

When choreographing for the hammer, you ought to incorporate a lot of evasion and handle parries into the fight if you want it to go on for any length of time. Otherwise treat the hammer (carried in one hand), mace, and flail as you would a sword and shield fight.

In writing about axes and other crushing weapons, I have focused on what you can and cannot do in terms of realistically replicating what a fight would have been like in the real time and place. The stage replicas you use will not be as heavy, as sharp, or as powerful as the originals. Those weapons had awesome power, and fights with them were brutal,

graceless, and short. The men of the time did not play Douglas Fairbanks (Junior or Senior) up and down the stairs with battle-axes. Dramatic license is a wonderful magic wand. You can and may do whatever you please and whatever your actors can accomplish, and your audience will be none the wiser, unless you are performing for the British Society of Stage-Fight Directors.

The power of these weapons, however, does impose an extra obligation on your planning when you take artistic license. When you get your weapons, check their weight and composition. How heavy are they? Are the warheads wood or metal? How sharp are they? Check and test them in relation to the strength of your armor and your shields. Be sure that the specific defensive weapons you have can absorb a blow from the specific offensive weapon you have without splitting or giving way. Most of the time they will not. They might hold up under a few blows, but by the time you get through dress rehearsal they may be chewed up badly and be dangerously weak.

My strong recommendations for choreography with this classification of weapons follow:

1) Make it brief (no more than two or three exchanges).

2) Limit defensive moves almost entirely to evasion maneuvers and handle parries.

3) Most important, be terribly careful that no blow is designed to land on the body of an actor, even with isometric control. Create the illusion, if you wish, by going upstage, but don't hit him with an ax!

4) A flight path that is anywhere near the head or neck is quite risky with that much mass and velocity. Keep those to an absolute minimum, and design the flight path with an extra margin of safety for the man on the receiving end.

5) Try also to give the recipient an extra safety margin by increasing the arc ratio to at least 3:1.

I like the way these weapons look on stage, and I try to design them into a fight. This said, however, please note that I use them as a stage-fight director the way I use pepper as a chef: I wouldn't be without it, but a little goes a long way! These heavy weapons appear, flash, horrify an audience, and then they are gone—the fight is over. I would start Macbeth and Macduff with spears, have them lose or break them and turn to axes, and lose them and turn to swords. That I can do safely. Thirty counts of battle-ax alone is too dangerous. If the weapons are accurate in size and heft, and have metal warheads, I would hesitate to choreograph a lengthy battle-ax combat between two professionals. With amateurs, I would refuse to touch it!

SUMMARY

Sword, spear, battle-ax, quarterstaff—offensive weapons all—each with a defensive capability of some kind. Shield and armor—defensive in design and intent—each with some offensive capability. The way you will use each item in your choreography will depend in part on its design, in part on the strength and resiliency of the construction of the individual piece, in part on the strength and dexterity of your actors, and in part on all of your collective imaginations.

In working with these weapons you will often have a conflicting set of desires. On the one hand, you will think of a splendid piece of business, or exchange, that will measurably enhance the dramatic effectiveness of a fight. At the same time, you will recognize that this very effective movement of yours cuts the margin of safety for the actors to a questionable degree. Whenever there is a conflict between "flash" and safety, please come down on the side of safety. If you cannot adjust it, if it is to be all or nothing, then abandon the move, and go to something else.

Use your weapons aggressively and inventively. You will be hard pressed to think of some use for a weapon or piece of armor, that is physically possible and credible, which was not thought of and used before you, on the field of battle, centuries ago. At the same time, plan the execution of those moves conservatively. A soldier on the field of battle often had to rely on his wits, his reflexes, and a lot of luck to stay alive and in one piece. That should not be necessary for the actor.

Chapter X

THE HANDLING OF FIREARMS

Most of the plays produced in the United States each year are modern plays. In general parlance this means they date from Ibsen to the present. Therefore, most of the weapons used in these plays (when any are used at all) are modern weapons, and that means firearms. There are a number of things you need to be aware of in handling firearms onstage, and these tend to divide into three areas: a) safety procedures; b) choosing the right weapon and using it on stage; and c) reproducing a realistic presentation of having fired, or having been hit by, a bullet from the firearm in question. This last involves body awareness of weight, recoil, and ballistic shock, from the actor.

SAFETY PROCEDURES

Perhaps the first safety procedure you should follow is to make sure you are not arrested before the gun is ever used in rehearsal or performance. Many states and communities have statutes about the registration, possession, transportation, and use of firearms. If your production involves the use of one or more guns, even if they are never fired, you should get in touch with the local police to make sure you are in compliance with all applicable laws. While it is not usually necessary for each person who handles the gun in the production to be registered and/or licensed, this may well be required for the stage manager or whoever is in charge of the weapon.

In most states a weapon cannot be transported while it is loaded. In many states it cannot be transported unless it is disassembled, encased, or both. These laws do apply to you. You will have to transport the weapon from the home or store where it has been acquired. You will have to return it.

Many states have laws about what type of firearms you may possess. Automatic weapons are illegal everywhere. Your script may call for the use of an automatic weapon. You may have a friend or relative who owns one he brought home as a souvenir from military service, or that he has acquired in ignorance of the law—or in defiance of it. If he owns it, that is his business; but you don't want it. Let us say you have a 600-seat auditorium and are going to give four performances. Do you want to display your commission of a felony before 2,400 people? Genuine automatic weapons that have been rendered inoperable in a specific manner, and replicas of these weapons that never were operable, are perfectly legal. They can be rented from a variety of sources. If you cannot acquire a legal automatic gun, I would recommend that you change the weapon rather than break the law. I have never known either a judge or a jury to accept "dramatic license" as a valid defense for the commission of a crime.

There are federal, state, and local statutes regulating the length of the barrel on rifles, shotguns, and pistols. The stringency of these laws varies according to geographical location. Sawed-off shotguns are illegal everywhere in the United States by federal statute. The same is true of silencers. Again, legal replicas are available to you. Find them, or make an adjustment in the script. Always check with your local police before acquiring and using a gun in your production. You may think the law is foolish or not applicable to you because you are "just doing a play." The first statement is a matter of opinion; the second is not. What could happen? A lot could happen. For example, your Uncle Harry's sub-machine gun, brought home from Guadalcanal in 1945 and lovingly cared for ever since, would make a perfect prop for *Home of the Brave* or *Bury the Dead*. But if it gets lost, or stolen, from your properties table, particularly if it turns up later in the commission of a crime, both you and Uncle Harry are in big trouble. If you feel compelled through irritation, arrogance, or the pressure of time to ignore the law on the possession of firearms, be aware of and prepared for the possibility of legal consequences.

When handling any firearm, make sure it is not loaded. I do not think one should ever store a loaded gun. Too many accidents happen that way. Obviously many people disagree with me. But a friend or relative who is perfectly responsible in all other ways may offer to lend you a gun as a property and then hand you a weapon with a live shell in the chamber or live ammunition in the clip. Whenever you take possession of a firearm, put the safety catch on and then check immediately to make sure it is not loaded. Don't stare at this page and mutter about my "being crazy . . . only a damn fool would hand over a loaded gun." If I seem hypersensitive and alarmist, it is because we do have thousands of gunshot accidents each year in this country, because someone thought the gun was not loaded.

Precisely for those reasons, never send someone unfamiliar with firearms to pick up the gun you have arranged to borrow. If your manpower selection permits, try not to put a novice in charge of a firearm once it has been received in the theatre.

When using a gun on stage, do not fire it at the victim from a distance of less than 6 feet, if your play text gives you any choice at all. Never aim the weapon at the face from any distance. If you must fire from close in, because, for example, the two characters are grappling for the gun as it goes off, make sure the muzzle of the gun is aimed completely away from anyone and everyone. You might also make sure that it is aimed away from any furniture, property, or set piece that you would care to maintain intact.

When a blank cartridge is fired, you are firing a bullet with the lead missile removed. You still have the gunpowder and the wad used to tamp the powder down and hold it in place. When the gun is fired, the powder explodes and there is a substantial flash at the muzzle of the gun. Flame, unexploded grains of gunpowder, and fragments of the wad are expelled from the muzzle. Anything within 6 feet of the muzzle is likely to get a powder burn. The severity of the burn will be in proportion to the bore of the weapon, the amount of powder used, and the distance of the victim from the gun muzzle. Again, stay away from the face. Powder burns can disfigure and blind!

I have never been witness, fortunately, to a gun accident onstage that involved an actor. I have seen some other fascinating occurrences. I have seen a gun carefully positioned to avoid burning an actor ruin a piece of upholstered furniture with the powder from the muzzle flash. Those of you with an interest in theatre history might remember that Shakespeare's Globe Theatre burned down when the wadding from a cannon became lodged in the thatched roof during a performance. They were firing blanks, too.

The larger the bore, or caliber, of the firearm, the more wadding will be thrown out of the muzzle and the more severe the muzzle flash will be. Shotguns are particularly dangerous. At the University of Wisconsin–Superior, we were doing a production of *We Bombed in New Haven*. The script calls for a character to be dispatched with a shotgun. We had a 12-gauge shotgun, double-barreled, in excellent condition. We were debating whether to aim the gun upstage of the actor or to give him a flak-jacket arrangement under his shirt and fire the gun into him. We test-fired a blank load into a galvanized steel bucket from a distance of 6 feet, and the wad from the blank blew a 3-inch hole into the bottom of the bucket. Needless to say, we fired upstage of him. We also cleared the flight path of the muzzle blast of any actors, furniture, or backstage personnel and set up a mattress arrangement of broad dimensions in the wings.

When you are forced to use a firearm close to an actor, you can rent weapons that have been specifically designed for the stage. These firearms have been built with a plugged muzzle and ventilation slots in the barrel that redirect the blast away (either down or to the side) from where the muzzle is aimed.

Never allow a firearm to be discharged with the muzzle facing the audience.

A firearm always has a recoil. Be ready for it. A .38-, .44-, or .45-caliber handgun has quite a wallop. If you are not ready for it, if your grip is not tight and your body stance is not firm, the recoil can sprain your hand or your wrist and jar you backward.

By the same token, be prepared for the recoil of a rifle or shotgun. You need to be braced to accept that recoil without going off balance. If you are firing the weapon from your shoulder, you also need to have the butt of the gun nestled securely, comfortably, and firmly into your shoulder. Bruises and soreness are common, even when the novice has held the gun correctly. The recoil is very strong. A heavy-recoil weapon, such as a 12-gauge shotgun, can cause a bone fracture in the shoulder or collarbone or a slight shoulder separation if held away from the shoulder when fired and allowed to crash back into it.

Never load a firearm until shortly before it is to be used. Never handle a firearm if you don't have to. The same rules that apply to the handling of knives and swords apply to the handling of guns:

a) Only the prop-master and the actor who uses it may touch a firearm.

b) Never handle it except to bring it onstage for use. Return it immediately to the prop-master after use.

c) Always carry the weapon muzzle down and with the safety catch on, even though you know it isn't loaded. An accidental discharge with a blank cartridge can cause injury.

d) Never leave the weapon in the properties closet, or on the properties table, while it is loaded. The prop-master should load the weapon with the blank cartridge no more than a few minutes before the actor collects it to take on stage. A loaded weapon lying on the property table for two hours, waiting for an entrance in Act III, is a potential disaster. Even if the wad and muzzle flash do not cause any physical harm, the sound of the gun going off in the wings is going to raise hell with your production.

Choosing and Using the Weapon

In Chapter VII I talked about choosing the right weapon for your character. I think we need not go into much further detail here. Sometimes the playwright is very specific about the weapon he wants the character to carry and use. If possible, follow his directions, of course. He may have been writing with a 6'2", 200-pound actor in mind, however, whereas your actor is 5'9" and weighs 160 pounds. His choice of a 12-gauge shotgun or a .357 magnum handgun may be a bit much for your actor to handle, and shifting down to a .410 shotgun or a .32-caliber automatic may make everyone more comfortable. Conversely, he may have specified a .25-caliber Beretta (à la James Bond) and it might look ridiculous in the hands of a huge leading man. Use your common sense. More often the text will simply refer to a "gun" or "revolver" or "rifle." Then your own aesthetic sense of the fitness of things has free rein. If you are not concerned with the visual image it presents, then a track pistol is legal in most areas, safe to handle, and makes a fine sound.

In looking for alternate and interesting ways to use the firearm, remember that you can do more with a gun than just fire it. The butt makes a fine weapon. With a rifle or shotgun you have available many of the tactics of the polearm and quarterstaff. If a bayonet is available for use, and is appropriate, you are still in a polearm situation. Realize that a bayonet can be used to slash, like a long-bladed spear, as well as to stab. In handling a rifle or shotgun like a quarterstaff, and planning blows with the butt, be aware of how heavy that butt is. It is an extremely dangerous weapon. A heavy impact with a rifle butt can crush in the target area. Show proper respect in your choreography.

BODY AWARENESS ON THE PART OF THE ACTOR

There are two people who must be aware of the characteristics of a firearm: the actor who fires it, and the actor who is "hit."

If you are firing the real weapon, then no acting is necessary to produce the proper reaction to the weapon's recoil. You just need to be ready for it. The same is true of the weight of the weapon. Often, however, a light .22-caliber weapon is mounted on a much heavier frame by theatrical supply houses for stage use. It looks like the larger weapon, but it weighs less and the recoil is very light. Where a mock weapon has been rented or turned out in the scene shop and is carried on stage but not fired, you may have a properties weapon that is much lighter than the real thing. Be aware of discrepancies, do some practical research, and adjust through muscle tension. This is an acting problem; it has nothing to do with safety and little to do with choreography. It can, however, make a difference in

the realism and therefore the impact of the scene. The actor who is being "struck" by the bullet has different problems. Thankfully, most of us have never been shot, and so we have no "resource" to reenact this on the stage. Some of the sillier moments I have seen on stage, screen, and television have been created by actors who have been struck by a .45-caliber revolver slug or a .30-.30 rifle bullet, and who have sunk gracefully to their knees while saying their farewell lines, and then keeled over slowly in the dust. No way! That was a convention that was perfectly acceptable at the time, but greater realism has been part of both our theatrical and cinematic heritage for many years now.

A friend of mine told me of firing his .45 automatic at an enemy soldier in World War II. The bullet struck the man *in the thumb* from a distance of about 15 feet and knocked him right off his feet into a cartwheel. The first film that depicted the true ballistic impact of a heavy-caliber bullet was *Shane*. When Shane (Alan Ladd) and the villain (Jack Palance) squared off for the final showdown, Palance was wearing a harness under his shirt that was hooked up to a series of piano wires on pulleys. When Shane's bullet struck him, he left his feet and was thrown about 6 feet backward through the air to crash into the wall behind him. *That* was realism.

It is both impractical and unnecessary for you to go to that extreme to create the illusion of being shot. But do try to avoid the "dying swan" act if you've been shot with anything heavier than a .25-caliber bullet from a handgun. A .22-caliber long-rifle bullet will stop your forward movement quite thoroughly from 10 feet. A .30-caliber rifle slug will knock you backward. If you were moving forward, a .32- or .38-caliber handgun would stop you. If you were standing still, they would knock you backward. Anything heavier, from either handgun or rifle, and any shotgun blast, would knock you right off your feet no matter what you were doing. There are variables according to your size, strength, and degree of determination, but those characteristics will take you only so far. I don't care what the script says, no human being, however large or determined, keeps moving forward after having been struck with a .45-caliber slug or a shotgun blast.

Acquaintances who have been shot tell me that the experience is akin to being punched very hard, or blocked hard with a shoulder in a football game. You do not feel the bullet entering your body so much as you feel the impact of it. That is, the sensation would not be of an object 45 millimeters wide entering your body, but of something the size of a fist, or even larger, smashing into that area of your body.

Allowing for adjustment for your own size and weight, the caliber of the weapon that shot you, and the distance from which you were shot, you should leave your feet. You will go into a front-, side-, or back-fall, depending on the angle at which the bullet struck you. The severity of the ballistic impact will be dis-played by the velocity of the fall and the degree to which you "roll out" the momentum created by the impact of the bullet.

Summary

Gun handling is a matter of law and of acting, over and above the questions of safety. These are matters for you to take up with the local police on the one hand, and with your director or acting coach on the other. In between there are real and serious questions of safety that may not be as apparent as those involved with judo or with knife handling, where the blade winks at you in the lights. A gun you are sure is not loaded at all, or one loaded "merely" with blanks, may seem much safer, a toy to be played with. It is not. Be careful when you handle it. Be careful how you handle it. Always check to make sure it is not loaded even with blanks when it should not be. Be careful where you point it, onstage while in use, and offstage as well.

Part III

THE CHOREOGRAPHY
OF CONFLICT

Chapter XI

THE NATURE AND TECHNIQUES OF CHOREOGRAPHY

In learning the choreography of stage violence, two broad areas must be considered. First there are the technical procedures for planning and noting down the choreography. Then comes the use of these procedures to create the finished choreography that will reflect and/or illuminate the character and situation of the combatants, and that will also create the desired mood and effect for that specific moment in your play.

THE TECHNICAL PROCEDURE OF PLANNING AND NOTING CHOREOGRAPHY

Choreography is merely the combination of ideas and techniques laid out in Parts I and II into patterns of action. From the simplest faint or self-stumbling drunk-fall to the most magnificent full-cast battle scenes in *Henry IV, Part I,* the planning and acting out of stage violence requires careful preparation and step-by-step instruction. At any given moment during a violent sequence, the performers should always know:

1) The angle and/or direction that he and/or his impetus has *come from.*

2) His foot placement.

3) The fulcrum of his balance.

4) The angle and/or direction that he and/or his impetus is going.

5) His physical relationship with other actors on the stage, as a source of motivational impetus (for example, has he been hit, shoved, or shot?).

6) The "flight path" of his weapons and his body.

There are several possible means of notation. The same rule applies here as in blocking notation: if you can read it and remember it, it is right. You can develop codes and keys in any way you wish, as long as they work for you. Again, please be on the side of conservatism.

You will probably want to use the standard positional code you employ for blocking notation: "X", "R", "L", "UR", "UL", "DC", etc. In hand-to-hand combat you could use "P"= punch, "S"=slap, "Ki=kick," "Kn=Knee, "E"=elbow, "B"=Butt. Thus instruction to combatant "A" to:

1) R.P. → stomach
2) L.P. → stomach
3) R.Kn → head
4) Stride in after him
5) Stride in after him
6) Stride in after him
7) R.Ki. → upstage ribs

against combatant "B" would be pretty clear. However, if your combat included both hand-to-hand and weaponry, some of the same symbols might be confusing. Does "P" stand for "punch" or "parry"? Does "punch" mean with the fist or the sword handle? Does "C" mean "stage-center" or "cut" with the weapon? By the time you finish inventing symbols and abbreviations for all the possible moves, I think you will have invented a whole new alphabet and/or language and will be so confused that it will take longer for you and your actors to encode and decode the fight in that manner than it would to write it down in plain English using full or abbreviated words. If the only single-letter symbols you employ are your standard blocking stage positions and moves, and all of your violence movements are uncoded English, there will be little chance of confusion. This is particularly helpful when your combatants are off in another part of the theatre with your notation in hand, rehearsing the fight. If your choreography is clearly and cleanly notated, like the examples that follow, the actors can work it out efficiently and safely. If your actors have to guess at the meaning of an unknown symbol, one can only hope they will be inefficient enough to come find you and ask. That way all you can lose is time.

It is my recommendation that you plan to write down your choreography "in clear," using full words or easily recognizable abbreviations. Use them singly or in phrases. You may shorten to single or double letter symbols wherever you feel comfortable with them, just as you do in your blocking. If you wish, add little drawings showing foot placement, hand position, or anything else you think will be helpful. The shorter and simpler the piece of action, the easier it is to use what would otherwise be a "cryptic" notation. The longer and more complex the business, the more I think you need to use full words. The most complex situation of all, where some twenty actors are having at each other with a variety of weapons and actions, is the one where you will be most tempted to invent a shorthand. It is also the situation in which a shorthand is most likely to turn into indecipherable gibberish by the next day.

There is another reason why longhand will work in the context. The more complex the battle, and the more actors on stage to participate in it, then the more time you should be taking between beats to check the six items listed above, particularly the questions of the clear "flight path" for the actor's body and for any weapon he might be using. This being the case, there should always be time for an assistant to write down what you are doing in a simple outline, or side-by-side chart form, such as those in the following pages, and to do so in full words and phrases. If there is not enough time, you are probably proceeding too fast for safety's sake.

All moves should be planned in beats, and measured out in 8-count units. If, for example, an actress is to rise from a chair, pause in fright, take three steps, and then collapse in a faint, that is an 8-count procedure. If she is to faint out of a right side-fall, it might be notated as follows:

Count 1 —Rise . . . weight on right foot
     2—pause for transition (see "the stranger" across the room)
     3—pause for transition (recognize him)
     4—stride #1 . . . on left foot
     5—stride #2 . . . on right foot
     6—stride #3 . . . on left foot
     7—start right side-fall faint, pushing off left foot
     8—resolve the faint by "rolling out" momentum to final position.

The point is the way in which the sequence is developed, and traced to its origin:

If she is to faint out of a *right* side-fall, she must have her weight on her left foot in order to initiate the fall.

If there are three strides before the faint, the first stride must be on her left foot, so that the third will also be on the left foot, thus correctly preparing her balance for the fall.

If the first stride must be with the left foot, then her weight must be on her right foot when she rises out of the chair.

If she is to rise from the chair on her right foot, then she must be able to get her right leg under her for support—if it was not there already—in time to rise gracefully and with full balance *to initiate the sequence.*

Violence, in this case a faint, does not begin with the moment of impact (counts 7 and 8), but with the initiation of the sequence of action that will lead to an impact. Thus, the moment of stage violence in question began when the actress rose from the chair (count 1).

Start with the violent business and work backward, step by step, to the beginning of the overall sequence of action. Plan from that initiating moment. If you do this, the performer(s) will arrive at the moment of faint, the collision, trip, medical seizure, or the first exchange in a fight with correct carriage, weight distribution, and timing and thus be ready to initiate whatever reaction to that moment you have planned for them.

The most colorful, exciting, and also dangerous part of stage violence is stage combat. The principles of planning armed and unarmed combat are essentially the same.

Unarmed combat (hand-to-hand fighting) provides the same problems and many of the same dangers as the use of weapons. It requires the use of the same procedures in planning and rehearsing the fight:

Step 1) All moves (offense) and counter-moves (defense) must be preplanned and worked out in detail and in slow motion. While you may desire an illusion of spontaneity in performance, as well as an illusion of death or violence, you cannot afford the real thing in the former case without risking the real thing in the latter. Spontaneity in performance should arise from acting skills, not surprise.

Step 2) Set up your moves, and divide them into beats. Structure your fight according to 8-count units.

Step 3) Rehearse each 8-count unit until it can be done flawlessly, in slow motion, five times in a row. Then go on to the next 8-count unit, again in slow motion.

Step 4) After the entire fight sequence is learned in slow motion (half-speed), the performers must memorize it. Both (or all) participants must learn, and be able to repeat, their specific action taking place on each beat of the fight. They have to be able to repeat it five times, without error.

If there are 22 beats to the fight, it will be taught and learned:

"1–2–3–4–5–6–7–8–; 1–2–3–4–5–6–7–8–; 1–2–3–4–5–6",

NOT

"1–2–3–4–5–6–7–8–9–10–11–12–13–14–15–16–17–18–19–20–21–22."

The shorter groups are easier to learn and easier to memorize.

Step 5) When they have given five flawless half-speed run-throughs, start them rehearsing at three-quarters speed. Leave them at that speed to rehearse two to three times per day, for a week. This applies equally to a two-man fight and to a full-cast brawl.

Step 6) When the cast can handle the fight sequence without error five times in a row at three-quarters speed, they are ready to try it at full speed. Be sure that "five times through" means just that. If they make an error on count 20 of the fifth run, they go back and start all over again, from count 1 of run number one. This is not harassment and is not meant to be an obstacle course. The idea is to imprint the sequence indelibly on their minds and muscles, so that the likelihood of error is brought as close to zero as possible.

Step 7) After they have learned the fight well enough to rehearse it at full speed, have them continue rehearsing it every day. They should do it once, without error, at half speed, again at three-quarters speed, and then two to three times at full speed *each day*.

Step 8) On days of performance, the actors must rehearse the fight at least once; preferably they should rehearse it once *each* at half, three-quarters, and full speed, just to make sure they have it down.

In a side-by-side chart format, a typical two-man hand-to-hand combat might go like this:

Cue/Line of Dialogue	Count	Jones	Smith
	1	Open door D.L. with left hand and stride in bar on left leg.	Seated on bar stool, back to aud., U.C.
	2	Stride #2-right leg.	Turn head to right (S.L.), see Jones.
S: "Hey Boy!"	3	Stride #3-left leg.	Swing around on bar stool.
	4	Stride #4-right leg.	Stick out left leg and trip Jones at ankle of right leg.
	5	Right-side front-fall starts here.	Sit on stool, and watch.
	6	Front-fall . . . full prone on ground.	Sit on stool, and watch.
	7	Roll out momentum . . .	Sit on stool, and watch.
J: "You shouldn't have done that, mister."	8	Roll out momentum, gather legs under you.	Come off stool, weight balanced.
	1 (9)	Rise with weight on right foot	Wait for Jones.
	2 (10)	Stride #1, to Smith, on left foot.	Stride into Jones on left foot.
	3 (11)	Block Smith's right hand, on left forearm.	Throw right hook at side of Jones' head.
	4 (12)	Bring right knee up into Smith's groin.	Block his knee by crossing with right thigh.
S: "I'm going to kill you."	5 (13)	Push each other off.	Push each other off.
J.: "You ain't that good."	6 (14)	Circle, look for opening . . .	Circle, look for opening . . .
	7 (15)	Circle, look for opening . . .	Circle, look for opening . . .
	8 (16)	Circle, look for opening . . .	Circle, look for opening . . . and see it.
	1 (17)	See him coming . . .	Lower head and try to butt him, drive in one stride on left foot.
	2 (18)	Step aside and karate chop at base of neck as he goes by . .	You've missed; too much momentum. Stride #2 of move, weight on right foot.
	3 (19)	Watch him go down . . .	Left-side front-fall (off right foot) is reaction to karate chop, start here . . .
	4 (20)	Stride to Smith, drop to one knee, upstage of him.	Fall is complete . . face down.
J: "You need some more?"	5 (21)	Watch him to see if he's "out."	Raise head and shoulders groggily, both hands out in front of you.
	6 (22)	Karate chop, again, to base of neck . . . very sharp blow.	Collapse forward, face down, unconscious.

A chart can be developed for a four-man fight as follows:

In Act V, Scene iii of *Henry IV, Part I*, the king's infantry could be listed as "K-1" and "K-2" and the rebel infantry as "R-1" and "R-2." All the script says is "Alarm to battle," but that usually means "Everyone on stage and hack away."

Cue/Line	Count	K-1	R-1	R-2	K-2
"Alarm to Battle"	1	Square off in neutral guard with sword and shield.	Square off, spear pointed at K-1's chest.	Spear pointed out at K-2; circle 1 step L.	Spear pointed at R-2; circle 1 step R.
	2	Sword cut to head.	Head parry with spear shaft.	Beat parry to outside.	Spear thrust at right shoulder.
	3	Shield parry at left flank.	Cut to left leg with butt of spear.	Whip butt of spear underneath and jam into K-2's stomach.	Double over R-2's spear butt.
	4	Sword parry at right flank.	Cut to right leg with upper end of spear shaft.	Backswing and bring butt of spear shaft into chest of K-2.	Give way in front of blow and go into a sit-down back-fall, drop spear.
	5	Bring shield across right side of R-1's head.	Fade before shield blow, drop spear, take a left-side side-fall.	Stride in after him on left leg and bring spear point into position to stab.	"Roll out" to left and wind up on stomach with your hands under you.
	6	Stride in after him on right leg.	"Roll out" to left, wind up on your back.	Thrust spear home, on upstage side of body.	Start to push yourself up on hands, be thrown back down by entering spear.
	7	Stride on left foot and thrust R-1 through with sword.	Receive and react to thrust between right side & arm: dead.	Withdraw spear, pivot to face K-1.	
	8	Withdraw sword with right foot on R-1's chest for leverage.	Arch body as sword is "pulled out." Then fall back . . limply.	Close one stride toward K-1.	
	1 (9)	Wheel to face R-2.		Close one stride toward K-1.	

and so on

As most fights are in two- and three-man combinations, you can develop a side-by-side format chart for as many pairs and trios as will fit on your piece of paper and on your stage and then simply start with, for example, "K-8, K-9, and R-8" on the next page or piece of paper. You can either put them sequentially in your promptbook, or tape them side-by-side on oaktag to get a "panoramic view" of what everyone is doing throughout the fight.

The point here is that "mass warfare" is simply a series of two- and three-man fights going on side by side on stage, either over-lapping each other or at one time. A cast of 40 in combat in Act V, Scene iii of *Henry IV, Part I,* consists of 12 to 15 such fights, each one of which needs to be assigned its own area on stage. You need to coordinate the traffic patterns of how the pairs of combatants enter and come together for their fight, and clear your flight paths for both weapons and bodies. But this is straight "crowd control" and is an exercise in blocking, not combat. As far as the "pitched battle" is concerned, you are doing a single two- to three-man fight at a time, and placing the separate contests in juxtaposition to each other to form the mosaic of your "mass battle." You control the tide of battle by the flow of the areas assigned for combat toward one side of the stage—toward one "camp"—or the other. This can give the feeling of one side advancing and the other retreating. You also create the sense of "victory" by the ratio of "kills" by one side or the other in the individual fights.

If you think of your large-scale battle as a mosaic, and take it one piece at a time, one individual combat at a time, you will find you can exercise full control over it, while creating the illusion of a fluid, formless melee.

Whenever actors make physical contact with each other, they should also make and maintain eye contact. Your partner's eyes will give you a clear and firm indication of his timing. They will also tell you immediately if he is lost, or uncertain as to the planned offensive or defensive choreography. That look of confused panic is unmistakable. If you see it, you have two options, both of which are preferable to injury:

a) *Tell* him his next move, even if the audience may hear it (i.e., "My right cross to your jaw. You're going down."); or

b) Disengage, tell him to go to the *final* blow of the fight, and then do it.

Sometimes you must forgo the advantage that eye contact can bring, as when a performer is struck from behind. In that case you must rely entirely on timing. In such a situation, be particularly careful. You have lost part of your margin for error.

When choreographing stage violence, you will simply be taking the techniques and moves discussed in detail in Parts I and II and stringing them together into a series of moves, countermoves, and reactions. All of the suggestions, precautions, and warnings that pertain in those earlier sections are still in force.

The more complex a fight is, in terms of either length or numbers of people involved, the earlier you should begin working on it in the rehearsal period. Even the simplest of violent business should be worked out in detail no less than four weeks before opening, and then rehearsed every night. If the fight is very complex, it should be learned as part of the very early rehearsals and given as much time to mature and develop safely as is necessary.

CHOREOGRAPHY FOR CHARACTER AND MOOD

Your choreography of combat always takes place within the context of the play. The combat is between two people. The fight itself will run from a few seconds to a few minutes, but the characters involved have been or will be the focus of audience attention for about two and one half hours. A fight is usually a climactic moment in the scene, if not in the play as a whole. It must be exciting. It must be dramatic. It ought to crystallize a conflict that has been building up for some time.

With all these ideas taken into account, the most important thing about the fight is that it distills the essence of, and reveals the innermost core of, the personalities involved. Character is revealed under the stress of combat as nowhere else. This is true regardless of the mood involved. The comic cowardice of Andrew Aguecheek in Shakespeare's *Twelfth Night* matched against the timid femininity of Viola/Cesario makes for an extremely funny moment in Act III, Scene iv. Falstaff's "dying swan" in the face of the Earl of Douglas

(*Henry IV, Part I,* Act V, Scene iv) is a comic moment that coincides with the desperately serious contest between Prince Hal and Hotspur in a battle where the throne of England hangs both literally and symbolically in the balance. Eddie Carbone challenges Marco with a knife (*A View from the Bridge,* Act II) in a tragic attempt to regain his honor and his manhood. Mercutio, Tybalt, and Romeo exchange blows and deaths in Act III, Scene i of *Romeo and Juliet.* The same fight between a bandit and a Samurai warrior is fought four times, from four different perspectives, as the characters in *Rashomon* search for the illusive abstraction of truth. These combats all vary in era, location, mood, intent, and in other ways as well. But they all have the one central unifying thing in common: in each of them the characters involved are revealed to the core of their being. Any pretense, illusion, or false image of their persons or their intentions that might have been present earlier in the play are swept away. We are confronted with the fundamental qualities the playwright intended us to see. When you choose weapons for your character, when you choose the way in which those weapons will be used, you must choose in terms of who that man is, what he has been, and what he will become.

What do you do with *Romeo and Juliet?* The combat there starts out as dangerous play between Mercutio and Tybalt and suddenly turns lethal. The mood is ambivalent. What really happened? You must interpret the script and decide. What mood do you want to induce? What do you want to say about each man's character? What kind of fight is it? Is it a classic duel, or is Franco Zeffirelli's rough-and-tumble street brawl appropriate? Is Mercutio's death an accident? (Romeo deflects Tybalt's sword.) Is it Romeo's fault? (Tybalt masks a "fair" thrust that Mercutio would otherwise have been able to parry.) Is it murder? (Tybalt takes advantage of Romeo's holding onto Mercutio and deliberately stabs him while he is helpless.) Which? Any of those

solutions will fit the dialogue. Further, what is the nature of the Mercutio-Tybalt fight that precedes the killing? Is it a pretty even match? All three resolutions will work. Is Mercutio completely outclassing Tybalt and playing with him? Though all three solutions can work here, this last approach lends itself to the "murder" resolution.

The point is that you have many options, and the one you choose will be for the purpose of creating a specific mood. If Mercutio and Tybalt go at each other playing the game of "King of the Mountain" with swords, then the sudden appearance of death is a terrible and tragic shock. If they go at each other with murder in mind from the first exchange, then we can have excitement and we can have death, but we cannot have tragedy.

What about the Romeo-Tybalt fight that follows? Do you want your Romeo to turn ferocious? He can. He can grab his own or Mercutio's sword, force Tybalt to a defenseless position, and then spit him like a turkey in revenge. This won't do much for his having a sympathetic audience in later scenes, however, when he pleads with Juliet that he didn't mean to do it.

Do you want him to be competent and romantic? Set up a fair fight, of some length; or an unfair one in which Tybalt outclasses him and must be overcome by main strength; or Tybalt "fights dirty" and is beaten anyway. This will be effective and not cost him too dearly in audience response.

You have a third option as well. Romeo can kill Tybalt almost by accident. In one production, Romeo picked up the fallen Mercutio's sword and screamed out Tybalt's name. Tybalt had run away in fear of the prince's reactions if caught at the scene of the duel, for the prince had decreed death as the punishment for just this sort of thing. Tybalt came racing back on stage, behind Romeo, and attempted to take him from the rear. He leapt at Romeo from behind. Romeo turned with his sword in hand—all but accidentally, more by reflex than design—and Tybalt hurled himself on Romeo's outstretched sword. It was a brilliant solution by that director, who wanted a gentle Romeo who could or would not kill at this point, yet had to follow the plot line.

Three different views of Romeo, Mercutio, and Tybalt lead to three different choreographies. As with all other movement in a production, the combat choreography must arise out of character.

We will examine specific combats in the above plays, and in some others as well, later on in this chapter. But first, there are two other contributing concepts to discuss: mood and rhythmics.

I noted above the diversity of plays that require stage violence. In Shakespeare's *A Comedy of Errors,* Goldoni's *Servant of Two Masters,* and most of Laurel and Hardy, and Abbott and Costello, we are presented with slapstick farce. People knock other people, or themselves, around with gay abandon. It is obvious at all times that the violence is meant in fun, and that no character (and no actor) is even seriously discomfited. There is a mood of comic adventure in Cyrano de Bergerac's duel in the theatre in Act I of Rostand's play. This time someone does get hurt. In fact, the Viscount manages to get himself killed, but we are in a semifantasy world where no horror is induced or desired—only admiration for Cyrano's mental and physical facility.

The combats in *A View from the Bridge* and *Henry IV, Part I* are serious and stark. Pity and terror, the classic cathartic aim of Greek tragedy, are the clear intent of the playwrights in both cases. The moods are diverse, and the means of achieving them equally so, but through the playwright's demand or your interpretation of his scene, at least they are clear. You know from the start where the fight must lead and what mood it must create, and you can set it up long before the contestants come to blows.

The mood, be it intense ferocity, gallant chivalry, or timorous hilarity, is your responsi-

bility. Please note that there is a direct relationship between the mood created and the nature of the mayhem that takes place on the stage. The difference is mostly one of perceived intent on the part of the audience.

Where we are dealing in farce and it is obvious that (a) no one got hurt and (b) no one intended serious injury, then a character can be knocked all over the stage, and the audience will laugh happily. Where we are in a form of fantasy, and the potential victims aren't real, where we do not know them, or care for them (they have been set up as pompous or vicious villains for the purpose of being killed off) then you can knock off one Viscount or sixteen pirates, or one hundred twenty of "the enemy" (in a war-play format) and no one will really notice with their emotions. The intent was to win, not to kill a person, and audience response will tend to be that of "Hurray for our guy(s)." The villains were never really human in terms of audience perception, and their deaths convey no horror, no pity. In serious, realistic combat—between antagonists we have come to know, and particularly if we have come to like or admire both men—a *human being* is being hurt or killed, and audience response is usually full and empathetic. If the perceived intent is to inflict pain or death, the audience will take that very seriously. Thus you must decide what you want to present to your audience in *Henry IV, Part I.* Do you want them to see symbols of the king and of the rebels in conflict; or do you want them to see live human beings in two different colored uniforms (tabards) struggling desperately to stay alive? That choice will dictate your choreography, two by two. It will also make an enormous difference in the way your audience will receive and respond to the battle scene.

Whatever your choice, the mood of the fights should reflect the mood of the play as a whole and be in harmony with the rest of your production. If you break out of context and stage an exciting fight that presents your characters inconsistently and violates your established mood, then you have damaged the overall production to gain a short-term benefit. It is not worth it. You are better off without it at all. Set up the mood of your fight to match the rest of the play around it.

Another factor for consideration in your choreography is the rhythmic structure inherent in a combat (or any violence) situation. The actors do not square off and pound on each other with clocklike regularity (as discussed earlier in Chapter VIII); the exchanges are *phrased,* instead. Rhythmics, however, has more to it than substituting an intermittent and varied rhythm for that clocklike regularity. This will assist the illusion of spontaneity. But there are also the matters of structure and of the tension that rhythmics can induce. Like all other beats in a play text, a fight has a beginning, a middle, and an end. The beginning phase, as opponents approach each other, take their guard, and begin to feel each other out— the pause and circle and feint that precede the first clash of steel or grappling of flesh—can be absolutely hair-raising if you allow it to be. This is a part of your choreography.

If the context allows it, let the potential for violence hang in the air and "steam." Stretch the tension until it is so tight it cannot stretch any more. Then, bring them together for the first blow.

Within this first phase, both tactical and psychological warfare is waged. The tactical warfare comes in the feints. The men bob, weave, make small thrusts, and fake their advancing "charges" just to see how fast, how well, and in what way their adversary will counter.

A series of feints may reveal to Cyrano that the Viscount is slow with a right shoulder parry and is vulnerable there. That is how he is able to "hit" him on that spot at will on the first try.

The psychological warfare is in the menace and the competency, in the overall impression one combatant conveys to the other. It is en-

tirely possible that the massive Earl of Douglas cows his opponents into submission with his size and noise before he ever lifts his weapon for the first blow.

The main body of the fight is in the clash of bodies and arms. It includes any pauses or breaks in the action—for breath, for dialogue, for agreed truce, for whatever—and concludes when one person has gained the upper hand and is assured of victory. This is the segment of the combat that requires the greatest degree of technique and control, for it is the segment with the greatest risk.

The conclusion or resolution is the deathblow, the knockout, the surrender, or however the contest ends. It often involves one or both of the combatants falling to the ground. Realize that the fight isn't over until the loser has finished falling, surrendering, passing out, dying, or whatever. Allow time and space for this resolution of the action in your planning. Also realize that it isn't over until your victor has acknowledged and reacted to his victory, and that too is a part of the fight because it is the complementary half of the resolution. The knockout blow, or the death-thrust is the peak of a very tension-creating moment. Give both your actors and your audience a few beats to "come down" off that peak and catch their breath so that all are ready to continue the action of the play.

Taking into account, then, character and mood, with the constituent parts of rhythmics and structure, there are three basic modes that you will find yourself in when you choreograph stage violence. They are: comic mode, serious mode—naturalistic, and serious mode—stylized.

Comic mode

Your first question might be, "Why didn't you divide comic mode into naturalistic and stylized as you did with serious mode?" The answer is that there is no such thing as "comic-naturalistic" violence, which is perceived as real. Violence culminating in genuine perceived injury or death is inherently serious, if not tragic. The depiction of violence is funny only with the introduction of some stylistic factor of intent, execution, or result that makes it patently clear to the audience that serious and/or genuine injury was not intended and has not been inflicted. This is the essence of slapstick and pratfall farce. Most people I know find the sight of an animal crushed on a highway to be saddening and even sickening. Yet these same friends—and I, myself—watch "Roadrunner" cartoons with perfect equanimity as the Coyote gets run down by trucks and trains, crushed by boulders and trees; blown up with shotguns, dynamite, time-bombs, and antitank guns. Why? Because we know he's not *really* hurt. He always gets up again, looking bedraggled, listens hungrily for the "beep-beep," and sets off in reckless pursuit of the Roadrunner once again. The Coyote is a cartoon character, not human and alive, and the violence he is engaged in is wildly exaggerated. Nonetheless the principle holds true. Arlecchino is not hurt by the slapstick applied to his buttocks and we know it. Therefore, it is funny. Ben Blue never was going to fall off that flag-pole, and we knew it; therefore, it could be funny. Comic violence is always stylized. It is an inherent part of the definition.

Comic violence is made up mostly of feints, slaps, trips, shoves, drunk-falls, pratfalls, etc. It rarely involves punches, knees, elbows, or kicks. The comic servant or underdog will often get a kick in the rear end, but this is a matter of placing the flat sole of the shoe in position and thrusting, as the recipient gives way in front of the "blow." The toe of the footgear just isn't used.

The three basic approaches to comic combat are the escalation of harmless exchanges into the destruction of anything except one of the adversaries, mutual timidity, and accidental dexterity on the part of the seemingly helpless hero.

The escalation technique has been demonstrated at its best by the Marx Brothers in their films, and by Sid Caesar, Carl Reiner, and Howard Morris in sketches on their old television series *Your Show of Shows*. The hypothetical routine is a classic and quite possibly dates back to Greek and Roman farce comedies. For example:

Cue/line	Count	Baker–Sid Caesar	Customer–Carl Reiner	Bakery Owner–H. Morris
C: "This meringue is too thin."	1		Holds pie out to Baker.	
	2	Runs 2 fingers through middle of pie & tastes.		
B: "No it isn't, here, taste."	3	Wipes fingers across mouth of customer.	One stride back on R. foot in indignation.	
C: "Oh yes it is, here, taste."	4		Stride on left foot and thrust pie in baker's face.	
B: "You're right."	5	Pivot to right to shelf behind to get pie #2.		
B: "Try this one."	6	Pivot back and thrust pie #2 in face of customer.	Catch pie in face. Stand there and steam.	Enter D.L., cross to center stage.
	7	Double over with laughter.	Cross over and get pie #3 from shelf.	Cross in one stride behind customer.

Cue/line	Count	Baker–Sid Caesar	Custmer– Carl Reiner	Bakery Owner– H. Morris
	8	Straighten up.	Thrust #3 pie in baker's face.	Cross second and last stride in behind customer.
O: "What's the matter here?"	1 (9)	Wipe pie off face.	Double over with laughter.	Try to tap him on shoulder but his bend takes him away.
	2 (10)	Get pie #4 from shelf.	Straighten up, eyes still closed, still laughing.	Withdraw hand and prepare to try again to tap.
O: "I said, what's going on?"	3 (11)	Thrust #4 pie at cust., over him & into owner's face on "ON".	Double over with laughter.	Try to tap on shoulder Miss it. Catch pie #4 in face.
B: "Woops"	4 (12)	One step back.	Straighten up and pivot around to see owner.	React to pie.
	5 (13)	Reach for pies #5 & 6; hand #5 to owner.	Point to owner and double over in laughter.	React to laughter. Take pie #5 from baker.
	6 (14)	Backswing with pie #6 at customer.	Straighten up, still laughing.	Backswing with pie #5 at customer.
	7 (15)	Thrust pie #6 past customer and into owner's face.	Double over again.	Thrust pie #5 past customer and into baker's face.
	8 (16)	React to pie #5.	Come up full front to audience, arms crossed in front of you, pointing at each of the others in glee.	React to pie #6.
	1 (17)		360-degree circle to left in reaction.	Roundhouse lefthand slap to right side of customer's neck.
	2 (18)	Roundhouse righthand slap to left side of customer's neck.	360-degree circle to right in reaction.	
	3 (19)	Roundhouse right slap aimed at customer but strike owner on left side of neck.	Squat: move straight down under the 2 flight paths.	Roundhouse left slap aimed at customer, but strike baker on right side of neck.
	4 (20)	Right-side side-fall: out cold.	Pop straight up again and grin.	Left-side side-fall: out cold.
	5 (21)	Roll it out to right.	Step over baker and take a pie from shelf.	Roll out to left.
Cust: "This one's good."	6 (22)		Taste pie meringue.	
	7 (23)		Step over owner and stride D.L.	
	8 (24)		Exit D.L. with pie.	

Of all the "mutual timidity" fights available in dramatic literature, the "combat" between Andrew Aguecheek and Viola (who is dressed as a man and calling herself "Cesario") in *Twelfth Night* is one of the funniest. There are no instructions from the playwright who simply notes: "They draw."

Cue/line	Count	Andrew	Viola/Cesario	Fabian	Sir Toby Belch
"They draw"	1	Draw rapier with right hand, throwing left arm across his eyes in terror so he "can't see it coming." Both are just outside of their swords' maximum range and cannot touch blades.	Draw rapier and hold with both hands in front, eyes closed, head averted, elbows against stomach.	Sit, well behind Viola.	Sit, well behind Andrew.
	2	Wild cut from R.-L. parallel to floor at chest height.	Wince at the sound of the blade through the air but don't move—just quake.		
	3	Wild cut from L.-R. backhand on same route.	Same as 2 but more so.		
Both: *Squeal*	4	Drop left arm and peek at her sword.	Turn head, face Andrew eyes open, and see sword.		
	5	left hand back over eyes.	Avert head again and extend sword to full arm's length.		
	6	R.-L. sweep; blades should meet about 6″ from tips.	Brace & receive Andrew's sweep.		
"Clang of Swords"	7	Drop sword.	Drop sword.		
	8	Pivot 180 degrees to R.	Pivot 180 degrees to L.		
	1 (9)	Stride L. foot to S.R.	Stride right foot to S.L.	Stride to intercept Viola.	Stride to intercept Andrew.
	2 (10)	Stride R. foot to S.R.	Stride L. foot to S.L.	Same as (9).	Same as (9).
	3 (11)	Stride L. foot to S.R.	Stride R. foot to S.L.	Intercept and catch Viola front to front.	Intercept and catch Andrew front to front.
	4 (12)	Bounce off Sir Toby's stomach, rebound 1 step.	Collapse in half faint in Fabian's arms.	Hold her up.	Grab him by shoulders.
	5 (13)	See Viola & shrink back against Toby.	See Andrew & shrink back against Fabian.	Grab Viola by shoulders and spin her 180 degrees to R.	Grasp Andrew & spin him 180 degrees to L.

Cue/line	Count	Andrew	Viola/Cesario	Fabian	Sir Toby Belch
	6 (14)	Resist but go 1 stride L.	Resist but go 1 stride R.	March her 1 step into C.	March him 1 step into C.
	7 (15)	1 stride more, same business.	1 stride more, same business.	One stride more, same business.	1 stride more, same business.
	8 (16)	Freeze & quake.	Freeze & quake.	Reach out & retrieve Viola's sword.	Cross into C. & retrieve Andrew's sword.
	1 (17)	Take sword very unwillingly.	Take sword very unwillingly.	Place sword in in her hand.	Place sword in Andrew's hand.
	2 (18)	Look at Viola.	Look at Andrew.	Retreat S.L.	Retreat S.R.
	3 (19)	Left arm back across eyes.	Head averted again, eyes closed, sword extended full arm's length as before.		
Enter Antonio: "Put up your sword"	4 (20)	Drop sword immediately.	Drop sword immediately.	Turn to Antonio.	Turn to Antonio.

There are numerous examples of "accidental dexterity." Some of them are evasions, as for example, when Charlie Chaplin absent-mindedly steps out from between two assailants at the last moment and they deck each other instead of him. With his ever-present cane, Chaplin as the "Little Tramp" was continually tripping or hooking his own assailant and sending him to the ground without ever seeming to have done it intentionally. This is the essence of accidental dexterity. The parry or evasion is successful and follows the same procedure as the serious defensive move, but the actor's motivation is different. The offensive blow (be it in armed or unarmed combat, and regardless of the weapon employed) is successful and effective. It follows the same balance, planning, and other safety procedures as the serious offensive move, but again, the actor's motivation is different. Offensive or defensive, he is bemused, befuddled and/or unaware of the havoc he is creating around him. He deals out crushing blows with sweet beneficence and not the first grain of malice. From the standpoint of the techniques of stage combat, he is in the same boat as the swashbuckling hero who is perfectly serious about his mayhem. From the standpoint of the actor, creating a desired effect, he is using a different style of acting technique and a different motivational pattern.

Serious mode—naturalistic

The serious fight in a naturalistic mode is the most common one, I think, and we have already mentioned several examples of it. When I say "naturalistic," I do not mean to limit the category to fights that are part of a contemporary play written in a naturalistic style. What is meant here is a fight in which the combatants are serious in their intent to harm each other, in which the weaponry or hand-to-hand techniques involved are employed in a straightforward manner to the best ability of the participants, and in which there is no attempt to poeticize the conflict or to make the conduct and action of the combat symbolic. The climactic duel between Prince Hal and Hotspur in *Henry IV, Part I,* is a case in point. Their confrontation is deadly serious. They attack each other with the weapons of their time, wielded in the style believed to be most effective by their contemporaries. Thus the conduct and action of the fight is completely naturalistic. At the same time, their conflict is highly symbolic within the context of the play. Held up before us, in the persons of these two men, is the fate of England. They symbolize the division of the realm, the contrast of two vastly different sets of values and life-styles. The whole question of who shall rule England, how it shall be ruled, to what end—all of this is compressed into and symbolized by this one duel. But that is play structure. The duel itself is almost always naturalistic in conception and execution.

Now, just to confuse the issue, one *can* poeticize the structure of the fight and make it highly symbolic of man's condition, while still maintaining a naturalistic mode. Again let's look at the duel between Hal and Hotspur. As the play and the productions have developed, there are a number of givens:

1) The duel is a battle for the throne of England.

2) The duel is a combat between sensible, statesmanlike moderation (Hal) and rash impetuousness (Hotspur) and thus is a clash of life-styles.

3) Man is a "bare forkt animal" (so what if the quote is from *King Lear*—the *idea applies*) and whatever his ideals and chivalry in normal times, when life is at stake man regresses to a total animal.

4) Hal and Hotspur confront each other after many "alarums and excursions," and so the battlefield is littered with the debris of battle. We have shields, battle-axes, spears, swords, flags, and standards in various states of disarray around the stage.

Now, let's see how the fight might go:

Both enter armed with a sword of war and shield.

Cue/Line	Count	Hal	Hotspur
Hot: ". . . and *would to God* thy name in arms were as *great as mine*!"	1		Assume neutral guard.
	2	Assume neutral guard.	
Hal: "I'll make it greater ere I part from thee";	3	Circle right, look for opening.	Circle right, look for opening.
Hal: "and all the budding honors *on the* crest . . ."	4	Shift shield to cover.	Feint cut to RT shoulder.
Hal: "I'll *crop* . . ."	5	Swing shield up and parry.	Loop sword overhead and turn "*4*" into a backhand overhead cut.
	6	Thrust at abdomen.	Deflect with shield to outside.
	7	Withdraw to neutral guard.	Withdraw to neutral guard.
Hal: . . . "to make a garland for my head."	8	Hold in position.	Hold in position.
	1 (9)	Circle to left one stride, ready to counter.	Circle to left one stride, sizing up Hal for attack.
	2 (10)	Circle to left one stride, ready to counter.	Circle to left one stride, sizing up Hal for attack.
	3 (11)	Recognize feint . . . hold ground & laugh, prodding him.	Dip RT shoulder, feint cut at left knee.
Hot: "I can no longer brook thy vanities."	4 (12)	Step to left and overhand sword parry.	Very large overhand cut at head.
	5 (13)	Shield face across Hotspur's head.	Fade in front of it. Left-side sidefall.

Cue/Line	Count	Hal	Hotspur
	6 (14)	Stride in after him on left leg, sword arm upraised.	Pull shield in parallel to body and roll left 1½ turns, taking shield with you. *Drop* your sword.
	7 (15)	Close with him. Advance left leg and overhand cut aimed at jointure of neck and RT shoulder. You miss and sword strikes the ground upstage of him.	One more ½ roll, 180°, takes you clear. Hal misses you. You are on your back.
	8 (16)	Stumble to your left, bruised & off balance but not injured.	Scramble to knees & swing edge of shield into Hal's right arm and shoulder.
	1 (17)	Recover balance, pivot back to face Hotspur; offensive guard.	Grab pre-set discarded battle-ax in right hand and come to feet, on guard. You still have your shield.
	2 (18)	See battle-ax . . . retreat to neutral guard.	Shield up . . . start to swing battle-ax in a circle over your head, building up blade velocity.
	3 (19)	Circle left, defensive guard.	Circle left, continue to swing ax.
	4 (20)	Circle left, defensive guard.	Circle left, continue to swing ax. Loosen shield grip on left arm.
	5 (21)	Catch & deflect shield with your own.	Throw shield at Hal.
	6 (22)	Evasion move to left so ax passes by your right side.	2-handed swing overhand at head, with ax.
	7 (23)	Pivot to your right to face that oncoming ax. Drop sword and withdraw arm from shield strap; grip shield with both hands.	Recover from miss. Bring ax head into position for RT. shoulder cut. This is one continuous move.
	8 (24)	Pivot complete. Set shield out in front of you with both hands and take the ax head in the middle of the shield.	The moving ax head continues, around on a right shoulder cut.
	1 (25)	Twist the shield and pull the ax out of his hands.	The ax is buried in the shield; try to pry it loose.
	2 (26)	Fling the shield and ax well upstage.	Lose the ax. Dive for Hal's sword, which is on the floor. This means going at least to your knees.
	3 (27)	Go for your sword. Too late.	Grasp Hal's sword.
	4 (28)	Convert this move into a bear hug of Hotspur from behind.	Try to get up and shake Hal off your back.
	5 (29)	Your right hand has grasped Hotspur's right wrist. Hold on; you are being forced to your feet.	Struggle to your feet forcing Hal up, behind you.
	6 (30)	Continue to struggle for sword. Get ready in terms of balance to go into a forward hip-roll.	Reach over with your left hand; grasp Hal's right forearm. Shift your weight to left to get your right hip into his abdomen and get right leg out for "ramp".

Cue/Line	Count	Hal	Hotspur
	7 (31)	Go into forward hip-roll. Let go of Hotspur's right arm as you "hit the ramp."	Take Hal over into forward hip-roll. You're using *his grip* on your right wrist plus your left hand grip on his right arm to pull him over.
	8 (32)	Roll it out. You have no weapon.	Pivot and start to pursue Hal.
	1 (33)	Finish roll . . . retrieve spear left in field.	Continue pursuit and raise sword for overhead cut.
	2 (34)	Overhead shaft parry with spear.	Overhead cut.
	3 (35)	Scramble to feet and RT. flank parry with spear shaft.	Right flank cut.
	4 (36)	Set up successful gate parry, spear point upward.	Thrust at left shoulder.
	5 (37)	Pivot spear butt under Hotspur's guard and swing it into his gut.	Double over spear butt.
	6 (38)	Hold spear shaft, parallel to ground and bring center of shaft down on the back of Hotspur's RT wrist.	Drop sword.
	7 (39)	Swing spear *shaft* in a cut against Hotspur's right arm and shoulder.	Left-side side-fall.
	8 (40)	Reverse shaft, bring point to bear and pursue.	Roll out fall. Come to rest on your back.
	1 (41)	Hold point *to* Hotspur's chest indicating "surrender."	Freeze.
	2 (42)	Keep spear point in position.	Relax, and slump back in seeming compliance.
	3 (43)	Follow him up . . . spear in position. Start to relax. You've won.	Start to rise, get both feet under you, on balance, halfway up.
	4 (44)	Be pulled forward, as you maintain your grip on the spear.	Grab spear shaft above the point and pull it past your body on your right.
	5 (45)	Fold over Hotspur's shoulder and let go of spear.	Jam your left shoulder low into Hal's chest as you pull him into you with the spear shaft.
	6 (46)	Stagger back one step.	Your balance is under Hal's now. Lift with your shoulder and throw him backward.
	7 (47)	Close back in and grab spear shaft. There are now four hands on spear shaft.	Start to turn spear to bring point to bear on Hal. Get halfway so that spear is parallel to both your bodies.
	8 (48)	Wrestle for spear.	Wrestle for spear.
	1 (49)	Wrestle for spear.	Wrestle for spear.
	2 (50)	Freeze spear, parallel to floor at face level.	Freeze spear, parallel to floor at face level.

Cue/Line	Count	Hal	Hotspur
	3 (51)	Loosen grip with right hand.	*Bite* Hal's right forearm.
	4 (52)	Lose spear.	Tear spear loose.
	5 (53)	Retreat 1 step back, trip, and do a sit-down back-fall.	Bring point to bear and come to a neutral guard.
	6 (54)	Roll upstage and come over a pre-set king's flags on a broken shaft with a spear point. You are on your stomach and on top of the king's standard.	See Hal and bring spear into throwing-"harpooning" position with both hands.
	7 (55)	Grasp broken flag shaft and roll over onto back, starting to get your feet under you.	Charge toward Hal, one or two strides. Spear held high and ready.
	8 (56)	Complete move to balanced crouch with control of the flag shaft in hands and your body masking the sight of the improvised weapon from Hotspur.	Close with Hal. Spear held high.
Hotspur: A vocalized cry of triumph.	1 (57)	Pivot, in crouch, and drive the spear point of the flag shaft "into" Hotspur's body, passing under his upstage arm, so that he is impaled on the flag of the Royal House.	Stop . . . raise the spear high to drive it home . . . then "receive" the weapon and fold over it.
	2 (58)	Press it home.	Drop your spear.
	3 (59)	Keep hold of that spear shaft and twist it. This is the deathblow. The twist is what forces him down.	Slow collapse to knees. Spear still held in place by your side & right arm.
	4 (60)	Withdraw spear.	Collapse backward, supported on one elbow.
Hotspur: "Oh Harry, thou hast robb'd me of my youth."	5 (61)	Drop spear.	
	6 (62)	Drop slowly to knees by Hotspur . . . combination of respect and exhaustion.	

The rhythmic phrasing and the exact angles of execution will depend on the director's taste and the actors' physical characteristics. The point is that a fight such as this can be highly naturalistic in presentation, and highly symbolic in effect. I rather suspect that many directors might find the use of the King's flag as the ultimate death weapon a bit too much for their taste. Really, any sharp instrument will do. Hal can take Steps 54 to 62 with a broken spear, a sword, a dagger, an arrow from a longbow that was lying "spent" on the field. Any weapon will do!

Naturalistic serious fights come in all styles, from all eras, and may be unarmed or may utilize all weapons ready to hand. The tavern brawl choreographed in an earlier section of this chapter is a timeless kind of fight and could take place (with very minor alterations) in an Athenian wine shop in the 6th century B.C., in a medieval tavern in 1500 A.D., or to-day. That fight is a workable sample of un-armed combat and the Hal-Hotspur chore-ography is a workable example of choreography with weapons.

I think you will find an interesting similarity

between these two fights, which seem so different on the surface. Naturalistic-serious fights are almost all "battlefield condition" confrontations. They may begin with ritual, but they soon become tests of survival where anything goes. Stylized combat implies some sort of ritual in its very definition and is therefore more likely to take place within some defined parameters, some form of "gentlemen's rules."

Serious mode–stylized

There are three concepts or characteristics that are most often present in stylized combat. Such fights are usually ritual, symbolic, and poeticized. Perhaps two of these concepts will be inherent in the situation, perhaps all three. A choreographer will want to decide which of them predominates in his particular case, and choose his approach accordingly.

In the martial arts films of the early 1970's, and particularly on the television series *Kung Fu,* the violence often turned mystical, and was practically always viewed poetically through the use of soft lenses, slight distortions of focus to further soften the impact of the rather brutal action, and especially by the use of slow motion. You cannot change lenses, or distort their focal length, on stage. But you can control the use of light and the flow of the fabric the combatants are wearing. Within our specific realm you can employ slow motion, or some other form of exaggeration or attenuation, as a poetic and/or symbolic technique.

The murder of Anton Schill by his fellow townspeople in the last scene of Durrenmatt's *The Visit* needs to be completely ritualized, or it does not have the formal "civilized" aura of an execution about it. The townspeople will be unable to justify it. They will fail, and the play will fail with them. Ritual violence is usually the violence of the state, or of some institution, against one of its own members. It is formal, neat, and precise in intention and execution—unless something goes wrong. It

tends to be solemn, ponderous in its rhythmics, and extremely impersonal. There is a sense of distance desired, almost as though no one is really being injured or killed, and no one (that is, no human being) is perpetrating the harm. Only the victim is allowed to behave in a human way. He is allowed to vocalize pain or fear. He is allowed to struggle. He is allowed to react. Of course the authorities prefer it if he goes along and keeps the matter entirely impersonal. Stoicism in the face of pain or death is a matter of pride in western societies. However, the sense of ritual is not broken if he struggles against, reacts to, or tries to avoid his fate. On the other hand, the moment the assailant (or executioner) displays a personal involvement by, for example, taking pleasure in his actions or displaying triumph, the entire ritual sense dissolves. The sense of the "impersonal many" versus the "outcast one" is gone, and we are back to a 1:1 relationship of assailant versus victim.

Symbol takes many forms. It can be a component part of a naturalistic situation, such as in the Hal-Hotspur combat; a component part of a poetic situation as in the *Kung Fu* combats; a component part of a ritual execution. It offers additional options, however, within the realm of *fantasy.*

When violence is cruel or so extreme as to be unacceptable, such as the putting out of Gloucester's eyes in *King Lear,* or the same business in Sophocles' *Oedipus the King,* then symbolic action is the only alternative to off-stage action. Oedipus blinds himself offstage. Cornwall gouges out Gloucester's eyes center-stage. If the actor playing Cornwall uses the technique described in the novel *Prince of Foxes* and by means of special effects creates the illusion that it has actually happened, then the audience will lose their dinner, and he will lose the audience. The use of symbolic violence will have a good effect here, without forcing the audience to choose between their involvement in the play and unacceptable emotional trauma. Given that choice, an audience will almost inevitably opt for their own sense of well-being and drop out of the play. If pressed hard enough, an audience will often seek escape through laughter, and the entire mood of the play to that moment will be shattered.

Another part of fantasy's realm in symbolic violence is where the reaction to violence is completely out of proportion. Once again the violence is not credible, but here, the lack of believability allows the audience to enjoy extreme violence because they are empathetically secure in the knowledge that it isn't real.

This is the basis of comic violence of the "Roadrunner" and "Laurel and Hardy" variety, where the reaction to inflicted violence is absurdly low in relation to the blow just sustained. It is also the basis of comedic violence where the bully goes into hysterics when he gets his toe stepped on or his finger pricked. Here the level of reaction is absurdly high in relation to the violence sustained.

The major area of use for this concept, however, is in the "action" play or film. Here the villain and hero batter each other in a manner that ought to cause immediate loss of consciousness, if not serious internal injury and/or death. Yet Humphrey Bogart, John Wayne, Steve McQueen, and company—and their villainous counterparts—keep getting up off the floor and coming back for more. This lack of appropriate and credible reaction tells the audience clearly that the level of violence is being exaggerated for their benefit. The violence has been stylized through exaggeration and is therefore acceptable and effective.

There are, of course, instances where the "violence" in the play text is completely symbolic; that is, no physical contact takes place. This can be tremendously effective. When Peter Brook had Charlotte Corday whip Marat with her hair in the Old Vic production of the Peter Weiss play *Marat/Sade,* he found a solution to that moment that was—and is —electrifying. I have never heard of its being done any other way. If a torturer stands in a

pool of light down-right and snaps his whip, while the victim stands in a pool of light down-left, some 30 feet away, and reacts fully to the imagined blow, once more you have symbolic violence. Both of these examples, however, illustrate a total use of symbol, where the imagination of the playwright and/ or the director has lifted that moment of the play completely out of the realm of this book. Where there is no substantial physical contact between actors, or between an actor and his stage environment, there is no need for the use of stage violence technique.

CHOREOGRAPHY AS AN INSTRUMENT OF REVELATION

If you are dealing with a well-constructed and well-written play, then each moment in it furthers the action of the plot and/or reveals relevant and enriching expository material. Everything that happens on stage points toward the illumination of the inner workings of a character's mind and emotions. These things are what drama is all about. The importance of a combat situation within the context and structure of the play, and the opportunity it offers for the illumination of character, have already been addressed in the previous section of this chapter. Given the same dialogue, the same basic action-solution, and the same basic facts about the participants in the combat, they may still be interpreted in various ways by the director and the actors. The way in which you perceive them as distinct and idiosyncratic human beings is heightened and can be ultimately defined by the way they react emotionally to the combat situation and by the specific techniques they employ (or fail to employ) in the fight itself.

Rashomon, a play by Fay and Michel Kanin, affords a fine example of this concept, for it contains four versions of the same event: the rape of a Samurai warrior's wife by a bandit named Tajomaru, and the subsequent death of the husband. The story of this incident is told by the wife, the bandit, the husband (through the mouth of a medium) and a woodcutter who happened to be nearby and saw the whole thing. Only the woodcutter has no personal stake in his version, but even here there is a question; one cannot be certain.

The Kanins have written detailed descriptions of the sword fights in their style, mood, structure, and sequence. The way the weapons are handled, the attitude of each combatant, the tactics employed, and the sequential resolution of each fight is already in the text, and I feel I could add little except form by choreographing them in these pages. What is interesting, and illustrative of my point, is the perspective of each of the four "deaths" the husband suffers, and the way in which the respective characters show their mettle (or lack of it) according to who is telling the story.

Tajomaru claims to have killed the husband in single combat. He depicts the Samurai as an expert court fencer—classic, effective, and disciplined, but unable to cope with a street brawler who didn't know or didn't follow the rules. "He fought very well," says Tajomaru. "Too well. Trained warriors should fight other trained warriors. In the jungle, they haven't got a chance." This image of the trained warrior overcome by superior cunning puts both the husband and Tajomaru in a good light— two fine, competent men—and it puts Tajomaru in the best light of all, because he won fair and square. He outfought and outthought the husband.

The wife claims that Tajomaru raped her and then left. She cut the ropes binding her husband with his sword, grateful that they were both still alive, but he refused to look at her or talk to her. In fury and frustration *she* killed him, she says, plunging his own sword into his body. In this version then, we have a murder, but no combat.

The husband claims to have committed suicide with his own sword, honorably taking his own life to wipe out the disgrace he had suf-

fered. According to him, Tajomaru walked away and his wife ran away. His version shows a beautiful and poetic death, highly ritualistic and utterly noble.

The woodcutter's version shows them both to be utter cowards and somewhat incompetent, and the fight described by the Kanins here is highly comic and resolves itself with the husband tripping over his own feet and falling accidentally on his own sword. Tajomaru comes off no better, having spent half the fight holding up his rapidly slipping pants, and much of the rest trying to retrieve his sword, which is buried like a rusty hatchet in a tree stump.

Depending on whose eyes you see them through, whose interpretation of events you believe, you see four entirely different wives, four Tajomarus, and four husbands. In no case would any of them recognize themselves in anyone's version but their own. It is a good play. Each version of the story pivots around the death of the husband. The nature of the three characters and their relationship to each other is first exposed and then resolved by the manner of his death. The moment of violence is the soul of the incident.

Perhaps the most detailed example of character revelation through combat choreography in this book is the Hal-Hotspur duel, laid out earlier in this chapter.

Hotspur has always seemed to me to be a marvelously vital, visceral man. He is intelligent but impetuous and full of animal vigor. He is animal force (albeit a charming and graceful animal) personified. With his human textures and boyish experiences fully taken into account, I find Prince Hal (destined to be one of England's most beloved kings, Henry V), to be a more cerebral, more thoughtful man than Hotspur. This is not to claim that Hal lacks emotion or even impetuousness. His scenes with Falstaff amply demonstrate these qualities in him. It is to say that, as I interpret the script, Hotspur's animal instincts and his emotional force often overwhelm his reason, while Hal's mind and emotions are in better balance, with reason usually predominating. This is my own feeling—not gospel writ. I tried to reflect that feeling about the two men in the 62-count duel I choreographed for them earlier in this chapter. Go back and look at it again. The core of both men is there (I hope) in the way they handle themselves and each other. Look again at count 51 and its follow-up. The image of Hotspur using his teeth in an act of desperation has been with me ever since 1960, when I did not use it but wanted to. Hal will dissemble, as does Hotspur—he would kick sand, scratch, and use any weapon he could acquire in any way he could think of—but he would not bite. That is the action of a visceral, animal, instinctually guided man

and it belonged to Hotspur. That act, ultimately, says a great deal about Hotspur and about why he could never win this battle or reign effectively were he to have won and someday have become king.

If your perception of Hotspur is different, then use different choreography to show that. But use it! Make your battle scenes exciting and they will fill the stage-time and the stage-space quite well. Make them illustrative of theme and of character and they can still be exciting, but so much more as well! Find the weapon that personifies that man—that is almost his alter ego; find the battle tactic that opens his soul to audience view, and your fight scene will be magnificent.

SUMMARY

Though the first section of this book is the shortest, it is also in some ways the most important, for it covers the fundamental and unifying action of stage violence. So much violence resolves itself in falls, and so many unnecessary, petty injuries take place in the act of falling. If you can learn to fall without hurting yourself in any way, then our time together has already been well spent. If your cast can walk away from the totality of rehearsal and performance time without a single bruise, abrasion, or floor burn; if you, the actor, can do this on your own, then your time has been well spent. Further, the control and awareness of your body, your balance, your stance, and your character, necessary to achieve a dramatically effective and physically proper fall, are valuable in themselves. They are the underpinnings of further success in the more complex realms of stage combat.

The basic techniques of violence are here in the book. Armed or unarmed, aimed at the body or the head, the techniques may vary, but the principles are the same. Start with kinesthetic learning as a way of life (and of continuing to live!) in stage violence. Practice —constant and consistent practice—is essential. Design your movement slowly, carefully, and individually. Take into account everything you can think of:

- The characters. ("How would he do this?")
- The actors. (Their bodies, reflexes, relative size, relative reach, sense of balance, etc.)
- The stage floor. (Soft wood? Hard tile? Will they pick up splinters?)
- The floor plan of the set. (Is there enough space to accomplish the action I want to do? Are there sharp edges of furniture, or stairs, or platforms to take into account?)
- The presence of other actors. (Do they endanger the combatant actors? Do the combatant actors endanger them?)
- Flight paths of bodies and weapons. (Do they endanger somone or something . . . including the audience?)

Now, rehearse it slowly and carefully for a long time until it is ground into the nervous system, the mind, the muscles, and the reflexes of your actors. Only then is it ready to be integrated into the scene. Practice on safety mats until it is ready to be performed in context, and then practice on the regular performance stage floor so that your actors are secure with the new and harder surface. Handle your weapons as seldom as possible outside of rehearsal and performance. Whenever they are handled, handle them with care and respect. These are the safety procedures— the mechanical principles of stage violence, to go along with the mechanical techniques.

Artistry is something else. As in all other art forms, talent cannot be taught. It can be encouraged. It can be nurtured. It cannot be instilled. To the degree that you already possess and display artistic skill in your work as an actor or director, to the degree that you have already displayed a sense of character and language and rhythmics and structure and picturization, to that degree you are ready to be an artist in the area of stage violence. The choreography of combat is an art form. The mechanics are in the book. The artistic capability to make use of them is within you—or it is not. Think in terms of character. Think in terms of milieu. Then, go to it!

There is an essential difference between stage violence and other performance or directorial ambitions. If your confidence exceeds your skill in any other aspect of production, the worst you will receive is a bad review. If your confidence exceeds your skill, or if "confidence" replaces careful preparations, where stage violence is concerned, the results can be much more severe. Actors are people. They are not cartoon "Roadrunners" or "coyotes." They are onstage live. We cannot yell "Cut. Take that again." Flesh tears. Bone breaks. Veins and arteries bleed—voluminously! Keep it controlled. Keep it careful. Then plan your fight as beautifully and spectacularly as your mind and imagination will let you; execute it with all the color and effect your cast can bring to it, and enjoy. All of you . . . directors, actors, audiences, and Blue Cross insurance companies together . . . enjoy.

APPENDIX

SOME AMERICAN SUPPLIERS

Robert Abel, Inc., 157 East 67th Street, New York, N.Y. 10021.

Castello Fencing Equipment Co, Inc., 30 East 10th Street, New York, N.Y. 10011.

Costume Armour, Inc., 381 Canal Place, Bronx, N.Y. 10451.

Eaves Costume Co., Inc., 151 West 46th Street, New York, N.Y. 10036.

Excalibur Ltd., 265 East Main, Centerport, Long Island, N.Y. 11721.

George Santelli, Inc., 412 Sixth Avenue, New York, N.Y. 10011.

BIBLIOGRAPHY

Ffoulkes, Charles. *The Armourer and His Craft*. New York: Benjamin Blom, 1912.

Forester, Amedee. *Roman Soldier*. London: A. and C. Black, 1928.

Gordon, Gilbert. *Stage Fights*. New York: Theatre Arts Books, 1973.

Hobbs, William. *Techniques of the Stage Fight*. New York: Theatre Arts Books, 1967.

Kelly, F. M., and Schwabe, R. *A Short History of Costume and Armour*. New York: Benjamin Blom, 1931.

Snodgrass, A. M. *Arms and Armour of the Greeks*. Ithaca: Cornell University Press, 1967.

Wise, Arthur. *Weapons in the Theatre*. New York: Barnes and Noble, 1968.